Valladolid, Oviedo, Segovia, Zamora, Avila, & Zaragoza: An Historical & Descriptive Account

Albert Frederick Calvert

Nabu Public Domain Reprints:

You are holding a reproduction of an original work published before 1923 that is in the public domain in the United States of America, and possibly other countries. You may freely copy and distribute this work as no entity (individual or corporate) has a copyright on the body of the work. This book may contain prior copyright references, and library stamps (as most of these works were scanned from library copies). These have been scanned and retained as part of the historical artifact.

This book may have occasional imperfections such as missing or blurred pages, poor pictures, errant marks, etc. that were either part of the original artifact, or were introduced by the scanning process. We believe this work is culturally important, and despite the imperfections, have elected to bring it back into print as part of our continuing commitment to the preservation of printed works worldwide. We appreciate your understanding of the imperfections in the preservation process, and hope you enjoy this valuable book.

THE SPANISH SERIES

VALLADOLID, OVIEDO, SEGOVIA
ZAMORA, AVILA, AND ZARAGOZA

THE SPANISH SERIES
EDITED BY ALBERT F. CALVERT

GOYA
TOLEDO
SEVILLE
MURILLO
CORDOVA
VELAZQUEZ
CERVANTES
THE PRADO
THE ESCORIAL
SPANISH ARMS AND ARMOUR
GRANADA AND THE ALHAMBRA
LEON, BURGOS, AND SALAMANCA
VALLADOLID, OVIEDO, SEGOVIA,
    ZAMORA, AVILA, AND ZARAGOZA

In preparation.

MADRID
GALICIA
EL GRECO
CITIES OF ANDALUCIA
MURCIA AND VALENCIA
ROYAL PALACES OF SPAIN
TAPESTRIES OF THE ROYAL PALACE
CATALONIA AND BALEARIC ISLANDS
SANTANDER, BISCAYA, AND NAVARRE

VALLADOLID, OVIEDO SEGOVIA, ZAMORA AVILA, & ZARAGOZA

AN HISTORICAL & DESCRIPTIVE ACCOUNT, BY ALBERT F. CAL-VERT, WITH 413 ILLUSTRATIONS

LONDON: JOHN LANE, THE BODLEY HEAD
NEW YORK: JOHN LANE COMPANY MCMVIII

DP
42
C17

Edinburgh: T. and A. Constable, Printers to His Majesty

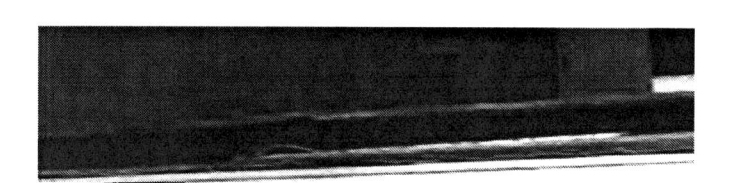

CONTENTS

CHAP.		PAGE
I. VALLADOLID	. . . .	1
II. OVIEDO	. . . .	38
III. SEGOVIA	. . . . . .	59
IV. ZAMORA	. . . .	86
V. AVILA	. . . .	103
VI. ZARAGOZA	. . . .	135

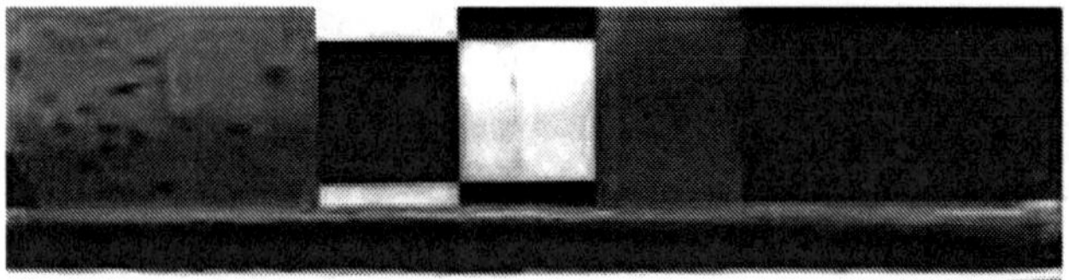

ILLUSTRATIONS

VALLADOLID

SUBJECT	PLATE
General View of Valladolid,	1
General View of Valladolid,	2
The Bridge of Piedra,	3
La Acera de San Francisco,	4
The Town Hall,	5
The Old Parish Church,	6
House in which Christopher Columbus died,	7
House where King Philip II. was born,	8
The Royal Palace of Philip III.,	9
Church of San Juan de Letran,	10
College of the Escoceses,	11
College of the Ingleses,	12
Interior view of the Library,	13
Interior of the Museum,	14
Façade of the Museum,	15
Museum: Back of a Choir Stall, by Berruguete,	16
Museum: Detail of the Choir Stalls of San Benito,	17
Museum: Several Fragments of Choir Stalls, by Berruguete,	18
Museum: Head of St. Paul,	19
Museum: Centre part of a Wooden Altar-piece,	20
Museum: Fragments of Choir Stalls, by Berruguete,	21
Museum: Fragments of Choir Stalls, by Berruguete,	22
Museum: Altar-piece carved in wood,	23
Museum: The Assumption of the Virgin, by Rubens,	24
Museum: St. Anthony of Padua and the Child Jesus, by Rubens,	25

OVIEDO

SUBJECT	PLATE
Museum: The Annunciation, by José Martinez,	26
Museum: The Holy Family, by Raphael,	27
Museum: St. Francis and a Lay Brother, by Rubens,	28
St. Joachim and the Virgin as a Child, by Murillo,	29
Provincial Museum: San Bruno,	30
Centre of the Façade of San Gregorio,	31
Detail of the Façade of San Gregorio,	32
Detail of the Façade of San Gregorio,	33
Left Angle in the Court of San Gregorio,	34
Gallery in the Court of San Gregorio,	35
Detail in the Court of San Gregorio,	36
Interior Gate of San Gregorio,	37
Façade of San Pablo,	38
Lower Part of the Façade of San Pablo,	39
Detail of the Portal of San Pablo,	40
Lower Central Part of the Façade of San Pablo,	41
Portal of San Pablo,	42
Detail of the Porch of San Pablo,	43
Detail of the Porch of San Pablo,	44

OVIEDO

SUBJECT	PLATE
General View,	45
Tower of the Cathedral,	46
Principal Entrance to the Cathedral,	47
Principal Gate of the Cathedral,	48
Cathedral: View of the Interior,	49
Cathedral: The Retablo,	50
La Camara Santa,	51
Coffin in the Cathedral,	52
Old Tower of the Cathedral,	53
Cathedral: Oaken Ark,	54
Cathedral: Section, Plan, and Details of the Camara Santa,	55
Cathedral: Cross of the Angels,	56
Crosses and Caskets of the Asturias,	57
Cathedral: Cross of Victory,	58
A Capital,	59

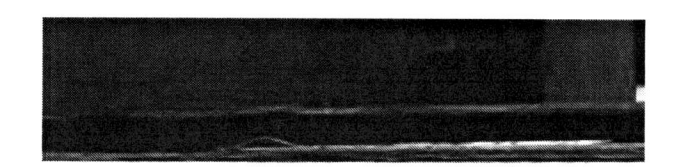

ILLUSTRATIONS

SUBJECT	PLATE
Santa Maria de Naranco,	60
Santa Maria de Naranco,	61
Church of San Miguel de Lineo,	62
Church of San Juan de Priorio,	63
Church of San Juan de Priorio,	64
Details of the Churches of St. Clara, St. John, and Our Lady de la Vega,	65
Details of Santa Maria de Valdedios,	66
Details of Santa Maria de Valdedios,	67
Details of San Juan de Amandi,	68
Details of San Juan de Amandi,	69
Details of the Church of Villaviciosa,	70
Details of the Church of Villaviciosa,	71
Plan and Section of San Salvador de Valdedios,	72
Details of San Salvador de Valdedios,	73
Details of the Churches of Priesca and Fuentes,	74
Details of Santa Maria de Villamayor,	75
Details of Santa Maria de Villamayor,	76
Details of San Adrian de Tunon,	77
Details of the Hermitage of Santa Cristina,	78
Details of the Collegiate Church of Covadonga,	79
Details of the Church of Ujo,	80
Details of the Church of Ujo,	81

SEGOVIA

General View from the Nievas,	82
General View,	83
The Roman Aqueduct,	84
The Alcazar and Cathedral from the Fuencisla,	85
General View from the Nievas,	86
Old Houses in the Plaza Mayor,	87
View of the Walls,	88
Aqueduct over the River Castilla,	89
The Cathedral,	90
View of the Cathedral,	91
View of the Cathedral,	92

SEGOVIA

SUBJECT	PLATE
Casa de los Picos,	93
Church of Santa Cruz,	94
Porch of the Church of Santa Cruz,	95
Church of Santa Cruz,	96
View of the Mint and the Parral,	97
Façade of the Parral,	98
Cloisters of the Parral,	99
General View of Turégano,	100
Turégano Castle,	101
General View of Coca Castle,	102
Another View of Coca Castle,	103
St. Andrew's Gate,	104
The Arch of the Fuencisla,	105
Gate of Santiago,	106
The Alcazar before the Fire of 1862,	107
The Alcazar from the Hoyos Hill,	108
View of the Alcazar,	109
The Alcazar from the Caves,	110
Façade of the Alcazar before the Fire of 1862,	111
Details of the Church of the Parral,	112
Church of St. Nicholas,	113
View of the Church of Vera Cruz,	114
Porch of the Church of Vera Cruz,	115
Courtyard of the Marquis of Arcos' House,	116
Façade of St. John,	117
Church of St. John,	118
San Juan de los Caballeros,	119
Church of St. Martin,	120
Porch of St. Martin,	121
Parish Church of St. Martin,	122
Details of the Church of St. Martin,	123
General View of St. Stephen,	124
Portico of St. Stephen,	125
Details of St. Stephen,	126
Church of San Lorenzo,	127
Church of San Lorenzo,	128
Lateral Façade of San Lorenzo,	129

ILLUSTRATIONS

SUBJECT	PLATE
The Church of San Lorenzo,	130
Details of San Lorenzo,	131
Interior of San Millán,	132
Interior of San Millán,	133
Arches and Eaves of San Millán,	134
Sectional Elevations of San Millán,	135
Details of San Millán,	136
Details of San Millán,	137
Details of San Millán,	138
Details of the Convent of Corpus Christi,	139
Interior of the Convent of Santo Domingo and Towers,	140
Painted Socles in the Tower of Santo Domingo,	141
Façade of the Convent of Our Lady de la Sierra,	142
Ruins of the Chapel of the Convent of Our Lady de la Sierra,	143
Interior of the Ruined Convent of Our Lady de la Sierra,	144
Porch of the Convent of Our Lady de la Sierra,	145
General View of the Roman Aqueduct,	146
The Roman Aqueduct,	147
The Roman Aqueduct,	148
The Roman Aqueduct,	149
The Roman Aqueduct,	150
The Roman Aqueduct,	151
The Roman Aqueduct,	152
A Dance in the Plaza del Pueblo de Nieva,	153
Enrique IV. conducting the Infanta Isabel through the Streets of Segovia,	154
Group of Peasants of the Province,	155
Peasants of the Province,	156
Peasants of the Province,	157
Peasants of the Province,	158
Peasants of the Province,	159
Peasants of the Province,	160
Peasants of the Province,	161
Peasants of the Province,	162
Peasants of the Province,	163
Peasants of the Province,	164
Peasants of the Province,	165

ZAMORA

SUBJECT	PLATE
View of Zamora,	166
View of Zamora,	167
Walls and Postern Gate,	168
Stone Bridge over the Duero,	169
Bridge over the Duero,	170
View of the Cathedral,	171
Façade of the Cathedral,	172
Cathedral: Gate of the Bishop,	173
The Cathedral: East Front,	174
Cathedral: Gate of the Bishop,	175
Cathedral: Gate of the Bishop,	176
Ancient Cistercian Monastery of Moreruela,	177
Ancient Cistercian Monastery of Moreruela,	178
Ancient Cistercian Monastery of Moreruela: Detail of the Interior,	179
Ancient Cistercian Monastery of Moreruela: Detail of the Interior,	180
Ancient Cistercian Monastery of Moreruela: Chancel,	181
Ancient Cistercian Monastery of Moreruela: Example of the Vaulting,	182
Ancient Cistercian Monastery of Moreruela: Interior,	183
Ancient Cistercian Monastery of Moreruela: Transept and Nave,	184
Ancient Cistercian Monastery of Moreruela: Detail of a Window,	185
Ancient Cistercian Monastery of Moreruela: Transept Porch,	186
Santa Maria la Nueva: Detail of the Exterior,	187
Santa Maria la Nueva: Doorway,	188
Santa Maria la Nueva: Capitals of Recessed Windows,	189
Church of the Magdalen,	190
Principal Door of the Church of the Magdalen,	191
Plan and Sections of the Church of St. Peter,	192
Details of the Church of St. Peter (Nave),	193
House of The Cid,	194

ILLUSTRATIONS

SUBJECT	PLATE
Tapestry of the Beginning of the Fifteenth Century,	195
Painting in the Town Hall,	196
Painting in the Town Hall,	197
Painting in the Town Hall,	198
Painting in the Town Hall,	199
The Royal Escutcheon,	200
St. Ferdinand and King John II.,	201
The Arms of the Town,	202
Queen Urraca and Aris Gonzalo,	203
Trophies of Arms and Armour in the Town Hall,	204
The House of the Momos,	205
Bridge of Rocobayo over the Esla,	206
Stone Quarries of the Town of Valderojo,	207
Earthworks of the ancient City of Toro,	208
North and Centre Gates of the Church of Toro,	209
Details of the Church of Toro,	210
Group of Peasants of the Village of Bermigo de Sayago,	211
Group of Peasants of the Village of Carbajales,	212
Peasants of the Village of Bermigo de Sayago,	213

AVILA

General View,	214
General View,	215
View of Avila,	216
Gate of the Alcazar,	217
Gate of San Vicente,	218
Gate of San Vicente,	219
Gate of San Vicente,	220
Gate of San Vicente,	221
A Street,	222
View of the Cathedral,	223
Exterior of the Cathedral,	224
Entrance to the Cathedral,	225
Plan of the Cathedral,	226
The Cathedral,	227
Side Door of the Cathedral,	228

AVILA

SUBJECT	PLATE
Cathedral: Pulpit of Repoussé Iron Work,	229
Cathedral: Pulpit of Repoussé Iron Work,	230
Cathedral: Pulpit of Repoussé Iron Work,	231
Interior of the Cathedral,	232
Cathedral: Detail of the Interior,	233
Cathedral: Detail of the Choir,	234
Cathedral: The Choir,	235
Cathedral: Detail of the Choir,	236
Cathedral: Detail of the Choir,	237
Cathedral: Detail of the Choir,	238
Cathedral: Altar of San Segundo,	239
Cathedral: Altar of Santa Lucia,	240
Cathedral: Sepulchre of Don Juan d'Avila,	241
Cathedral: Tomb of El Testado,	242
Cathedral: Altar behind the Choir,	243
Cathedral: Silver Monstrance of Juan de Arfe,	244
Convent of Santo Tomas: Sepulchre of the Infante Don Juan,	245
Sepulchre of the Holy Martyrs Vicente, Sabina, and Cristina,	246
Interior of the Chapel of San Bernardo,	247
Church of St. Peter,	248
Entrance to the Church of St. Peter,	249
Church of St. Peter,	250
Details of the Church of St. Peter,	251
Exterior of the Church of San Vicente,	252
Basilica of San Vicente before its restoration,	253
Basilica of San Vicente before its restoration,	254
Basilica of San Vicente: North Façade,	255
Basilica of San Vicente: Principal Façade,	256
Basilica of San Vicente: Eastern Façade, restored,	257
Basilica of San Vicente: Façade,	258
Basilica of San Vicente: Central Gate, restored,	259
Basilica of San Vicente: Detail of the middle cornice, restored,	260
Basilica of San Vicente: Portal,	261
Basilica of San Vicente: Principal west entrance,	262
Basilica of San Vicente: Principal west entrance,	263
Basilica of San Vicente: General view of the Interior,	264
Basilica of San Vicente: Sepulchre of the Holy Martyrs,	265

ILLUSTRATIONS

SUBJECT	PLATE
Basilica of San Vicente: Detail of the Interior,	266
Porch of the Church of San Vicente,	267
Porch of the Church of San Vicente,	268
Porch of the Convent of Santo Tomas,	269
Section of the Convent of Santo Tomas,	270
Plan of the Convent of Santo Tomas,	271
Gate of the Convent of Santo Tomas,	272
Door of the Convent of Santo Tomas,	273
Interior of the Convent of Santo Tomas,	274
The Court of Silence in the Convent of Santo Tomas,	275
Convent of Santo Tomas: The Court of Silence,	276
Convent of Santo Tomas: The Court of the Kings,	277
Convent of Santo Tomas: Courtyard of the Infirmary,	278
Cloisters of the Convent of Santo Tomas,	279
Cloisters of the Convent of Santo Tomas,	280
Cloisters of the Convent of Santo Tomas,	281
Gate of the Cloisters in the Convent of Santo Tomas,	282
Choir of the Convent of Santo Tomas,	283
Convent of Santo Tomas: Details of the Choir,	284
Choir Stalls in the Convent of Santo Tomas,	285
Choir Stalls in the Convent of Santo Tomas,	286
Church of San Segundo: Statue of San Segundo,	287
Church of Santo Tomas: Sepulchre of the Infante Don Juan,	288
Church of Santo Tomas: Sepulchre of the Infante Don Juan,	289
Church of Santo Tomas: Sepulchre of the Infante Don Juan,	290
Gothic Gate in ruins,	291
Door of a Private House,	292
Calle de Pedro d'Avila,	293
Celebrated Window in the House of Pedro d'Avila,	294
Courtyard of the Polentinos' Palace,	295
Portico of the Polentinos' Palace,	296
Church of San Andrés and San Segundo,	297
Hermitage of San Isidro,	298
The Academy,	299
Camposagrado Palace,	300
Casa de la Baraganas,	301
Casa de la Torre,	302

ZARAGOZA

SUBJECT	PLATE
Chapel of Mosen Rubi,	303
Palace of the Conde de Superunda,	304
Miniatures from the Avila Missal,	305
Miniatures from the Avila Missal,	306
Door of San Francisco,	307
A Roman Capital of the Church of San Franciso,	308
Latin-Byzantine Frieze in the Church of San Francisco,	309
Monastery of San Pedro at Arenas,	310

ZARAGOZA

General View from Cabezo-Cortado,	311
General View from Altabas,	312
General View from Altabas,	313
The Bridge over the Ebro, from the Ruins of San Lazaro,	314
The Bridge over the Ebro, from El Pilar,	315
General View of Zaragoza,	316
General View of Zaragoza,	317
General View of Zaragoza,	318
General View from the Portilla,	319
View of Zaragoza,	320
Calle del Mercado,	321
Paseo de Santa Engracia,	322
Cathedral of La Seo,	323
Cathedral of La Seo,	324
Glazed Tiles on the Walls of the Cathedral of La Seo,	325
Interior of the Cathedral of La Seo,	326
Cathedral of La Seo: View of the Transept,	327
Cathedral of La Seo: Detail of Transept,	328
Chapel of St. John in the Cathedral of La Seo,	329
Chapel of Gabriel de Zaporta in the Cathedral of La Seo,	330
Cathedral of La Seo: Reja bronze repoussé,	331
Sepulchre of Archbishop Don Lope de Luna in the Cathedral of La Seo,	332
Central Dome of the Cathedral of La Seo,	333
Silver Monstrance in the Cathedral of La Seo,	334

ILLUSTRATIONS xxi

SUBJECT	PLATE
Censer belonging to the Cathedral of La Seo,	335
Cathedral of El Pilar,	336
Cathedral of El Pilar,	337
Interior of Our Lady del Pilar,	338
Side Altar in Our Lady del Pilar,	339
Our Lady del Pilar: View of the Choir,	340
Our Lady del Pilar: Organ in the Choir,	341
Chapel in Our Lady del Pilar,	342
High Altar in Our Lady del Pilar,	343
Paintings on the Cupola of Our Lady del Pilar,	344
Our Lady del Pilar: Choir Stalls,	345
Our Lady del Pilar: Choir Stalls,	346
Our Lady del Pilar: Choir Stalls,	347
Our Lady del Pilar, by M. de Unceta,	348
Our Lady del Pilar,	349
Silver Salver in the Cathedral of El Pilar,	350
Vase in the Cathedral of El Pilar,	351
Church of the Magdalen,	352
Place and Church of St. Nicholas,	353
Portal of the Church of San Miguel,	354
Façade of the Church of Santa Engracia,	355
Church of St. Paul: Puerta del Cristo,	356
The New, or Leaning Tower,	357
Tower of the Calle de Antonio Perez,	358
Tower of San Miguel,	359
Tower of San Pablo,	360
Tower of the Trovador,	361
Ancient Wall and Buildings,	362
Statue of Pignatelli,	363
Courtyard in the House of Pardo,	364
Detail of the Courtyard in the House of Pardo,	365
Entrance to the Audiencia Palace,	366
Palace of the Provincial Deputation,	367
Courtyard in the Count of Argillo's House,	368
Eaves on the House of the Conde de Argillo,	369
Courtyard in the Count of Argillo's House,	370
House in the Plaza de San Carlos,	371

SUBJECT	PLATE
The Exchange,	372
Façade of the Exchange,	373
Interior of the Exchange,	374
Porch of the House of Zaporta,	375
Courtyard of the House of Zaporta,	376
Courtyard of the House of Zaporta,	377
Courtyard of the House of Zaporta,	378
Courtyard of the House of Zaporta,	379
Courtyard of the House of Zaporta,	380
Detail of the Courtyard of the House of Zaporta,	381
Court of the Provincial Museum,	382
Gallery in the Provincial Museum,	383
The Aljaferia or Citadel. Window of the Main Staircase,	384
Aljaferia: Interior of the Mosque,	385
Aljaferia: Interior of the Mosque,	386
Aljaferia: Interior of the Mosque,	387
Aljaferia: Details of the Interior,	388
Aljaferia: Details of the Interior,	389
Details of the Aljaferia,	390
Details of the Aljaferia,	391
St. Isabel and her Husband. Tapestry in the University,	392
View of the Barracks of the Aljaferia,	393
The Casa de la Infanta. 'The Departure for the Fight,' by P. Gonzalvo Perez,	394
Gate of Our Lady del Carmen,	395
The Defence of Zaragoza in 1809, by Nicolas Mejia,	396
The First Siege of Zaragoza, by A. Ferrant y Fischermans,	397
Heroic Defence of the Tower of St. Augustine at Zaragoza in the War of Independence, by C. Alvarez Dumont,	398
Heroic Combat in the Pulpit of the Church of San Augustin at Zaragoza in 1809, by C. Alvarez Dumont,	399
The Maid of Zaragoza, by M. Hiraldez Acosta,	400
The Maid of Zaragoza, by Navarro y Canizares,	401
Arch from the Aljaferia Palace, now in the Archæological Museum,	402
Arch from the Aljaferia Palace, now in the Archæological Museum,	403

ILLUSTRATIONS

SUBJECT	PLATE
Provincial Museum: Detail of 'The Mosque' of the Aljaferia,	404
Provincial Museum: Corbels of Eaves, Gothic style, from the old Custom House,	405
Provincial Museum: Corbels of Eaves,	406
Provincial Museum: Corbels of Eaves, Gothic style,	407
Provincial Museum: Corbels of Eaves, Pointed style,	408
Provincial Museum: Arab Capitals of the Aljaferia Castle,	409
Provincial Museum: Arab Capitals from the Aljaferia,	410
Provincial Museum: Arab Capitals from the Aljaferia,	411
The Story of Lucretia. A Plate from the work entitled 'Mugeres Ilustres,' translated from Boccaccio,	412
A Page from the work entitled 'Example against the Deception and Perils of the World,' by Juan de Capua,	413

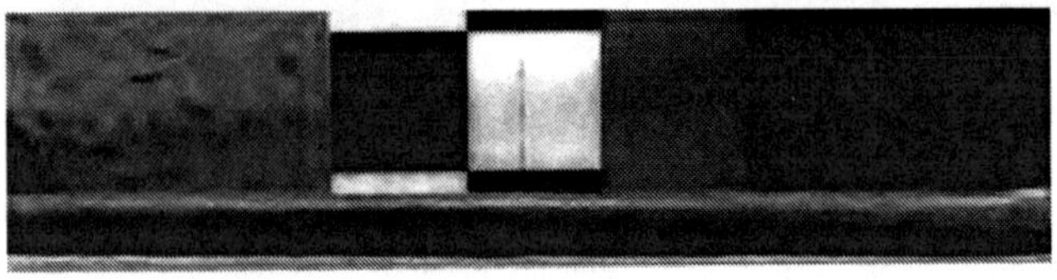

PREFACE

THE six cities of Spain which form the subject of the following pages are little known to English travellers. Yet no one who would understand the country can afford to pass them by. Not only are they compact of artistic and architectural treasures, but within their walls much of the history of the Spanish nation has been made. Oviedo—that little city between the mountains and the sea, so far off the beaten track—was the cradle of the monarchy, the residence and burial-place of its patriot kings. For all men of Spanish blood it is holy ground. In Zamora we have the typical city of the heroic age of Spain, the era of half-fabulous heroes, whose personalities are made known to us only by folklore and ballads.

Segovia and Avila are towns of the Reconquest, wardens, one might say, against the redoubtable Moor. To the fancy their grass-grown streets still re-echo with the tramp of armed men, with the ring of spears and the word of command. The shadowy warriors of Oviedo and Zamora here give place to the tall knight who stalks across the page of history, ready to do battle with pagan Moor or Christian tyrant. But Avila enshrines the holier memory of the sainted Theresa, greatest of Spanish women, revered not least in the lands for whose conversion to her faith she unceasingly prayed. And so we pass on, each town illustrating a different stage of a great nation's development.

In Valladolid, which preceded and subsequently nearly supplanted Madrid as the capital of Spain, we are again on holy ground; for Cervantes dwelt here, and here died the immortal Columbus. Zaragoza, the chief city of a kingdom that influenced the destinies of powerful European States when Castile was hardly known to the outside world, has ever been a noble and important capital, boasting a glory which has been brightest perhaps in its later days. To the citizens of Zaragoza was reserved the honour of rejecting the Inquisition, to which other towns reluctantly submitted, and just one hundred years ago she proved to an astonished Europe that within her crumbling walls dwelt the old brood of Numantia—that she was prolific still of heroes and heroines.

The prowess of Augustina would not indeed have come as a surprise to those who knew her country well; nor could the most thoughtless of travellers, after a survey of the memorials of genius and vitality which these six cities contain, ever believe the greatness of the people to be exhausted. Already Valladolid and Zaragoza throb with life and commerce. But a few more years and the other cities, already stirring, will pulsate with the spirit of young Spain, and the Phœnix, born a thousand years ago at Oviedo, will renew its youth for the tenth time.

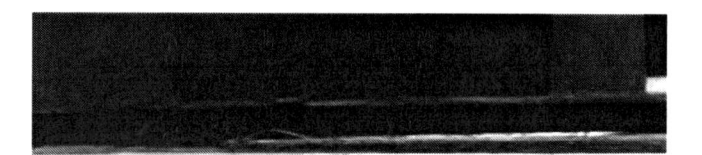

To Señor J. Lacoste my thanks are due for his courtesy in permitting me to reproduce many of the photographs which find a place in this book, and I have also to acknowledge the assistance rendered me by Mr. E. B. d'Auvergne in the preparation of the text.

A. F. C.

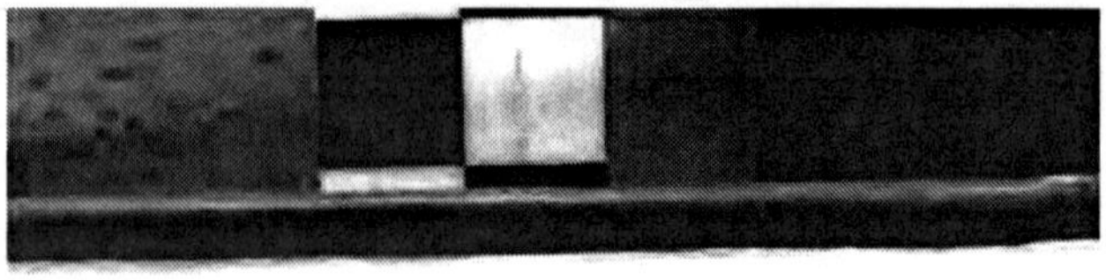

Valladolid, Oviedo, Segovia, Zamora, Avila, and Zaragoza

I

VALLADOLID

ITS STORY

VALLADOLID, a thriving, bustling place, as Spanish cities go, stands on the rivers Pisuerga and Esgueva, a few miles above the confluence of their united streams with the Duero. All round spreads the vast, dreary plain of Castile, interrupted within sight of the town by a ring of low hills. Trains thunder past from north, south, and west, keeping Valladolid in close touch with Madrid, with France, with Portugal, and with the rest of the world. The natural centre, this, of the old kingdom of Leon and Castile, of which it was for a long time the political capital.

The etymology of the name has perplexed historians not a little. The most probable derivation is from the Arabic Belad-Walid, the valley of Walid, or (as likely) of the Wali or governor. In Latin documents the name is Vallisoletum, from which the poetical etymology, *vallis odoris*, was ingeniously manufactured. Though a great many of the towns in this part of Spain were founded on fresh sites on the resettlement of the country in the ninth and tenth centuries, Valladolid can, with some show of probability, claim a more remote origin. The contention of the old writers that this was the town called Pintia, described by Ptolemy as lying on the road from Caesaraugusta to Asturica, is to some extent borne out by numerous remains, attesting the existence at this spot of a Roman community of opulence and importance.

The earliest mention of the place since the Christian era occurs in the Chronicle of Cardeña, where in the year 1072 it is referred to as one of the two towns (Rio Seco being the other) offered to Doña Urraca by her brother, Sancho, in exchange for Zamora. We may presume, therefore, that it was already a place of some consequence. In 1074 it was handed over by Alfonso VI. to Count Pedro Ansúrez, the companion of his exile at Toledo. This noble plays the same part in its history as Count Raymond does in that of Salamanca. The principal buildings, such as Santa Maria la Antigua and the bridge over the Pisuerga, are ascribed to him. He founded and generously endowed the collegiate church of Santa Maria la Mayor, with the adjacent abbey, of which, in after years, infantes and the sons of the most exalted persons were alone deemed worthy to be abbots. The famous Bernard, Archbishop of Toledo, came to bless the church, with the not less famous Alvar Fañez, who was Count Pedro's son-in-law. When good King Alfonso passed away, Ansúrez took the oath of allegiance to his daughter, Queen Urraca, and to her husband, 'The Battler of Aragon.' When the royal twain came to blows, the count surrendered all the strongholds he held to the queen, and presented himself to the king, saying that 'with the hands, the tongue, and the body which had paid him homage,' he could do as he willed. Alfonso the Battler let him depart unmolested, and he was laid to rest in 1118, clothed in his armour, in the collegiate church he had endowed.

The lordship of Valladolid now passed to Armengol, son of Count Pedro's eldest daughter, by the Count of Urgel. Under his sway the city prospered exceedingly. King Alfonso VII.

chose it for the place of his marriage with a Polish princess, and for several ecclesiastical councils. Two more counts of the same name continued the dynasty of Ansúrez till the year 1208; but of these the town saw little, for as Counts of Urgel they were vassals of Aragon, and spent most of their time in that kingdom. The last count left half of his Castilian dominions to the Pope, the other half to his daughter Aurembiax, who was believed to be the mistress of the King of Aragon. Alfonso VIII. of Castile can hardly, therefore, be blamed for setting aside a disposition which handed over the principal town in his kingdom to two foreign potentates. In the year 1208, accordingly, the city was incorporated with the monarchy. Soon after (1215) it became for the first time the royal residence—that of the Queen-Regent Berenguela and her youthful charge, Don Enrique I.; and in accordance with this precedent, two years later, Fernando III. was crowned here, in the Plaza Mayor. Thenceforward the town became the usual seat of the court, though an official capital in the modern sense Spain did not possess till Philip II.'s time. The last years of the thirteenth century saw the reins of government in the hands of a native of Valladolid, the Queen-Regent, Maria de

Molina, widow of Sancho el Bravo. Her predilection for her own birthplace practically extinguished the pretensions of Burgos to rank as capital, and during her stormy regency Valladolid stood by her loyally. She was not the least capable or intrepid of the many able women-rulers by whom Spain has been so well served.

Though the seat of government, Valladolid was not wanting in the turbulent, independent spirit characteristic of the Castilian cities. In 1328 a rumour spread abroad that the king's Jewish treasurer, Joseph, was about to carry off the Infanta Leonor, and to marry her to the detested favourite, Nuñez Osorio. Sure enough the princess presently appeared, mounted and attended by an escort, as if proceeding on a journey. The citizens forced her to return to the palace, and clamoured for the head of the treasurer. Leonor promised to satisfy them if they would permit her to go to the Alcazar, or citadel, whither she contrived to convey the trembling Hebrew concealed among her retinue. Safe inside the fortress, Infanta and Jew set the mob at defiance, and sustained a siege till relieved by the king. Comically enough, Alfonso dismissed his favourite on the ground that he was the cause of these disturbances, while the

Infanta married the Prince of Portugal, whom she had been on her way to meet when forced back by the crowd.

Women figure largely in the history of Valladolid. Here in the church of Santa Maria la Mayor, Peter the Cruel was married to the hapless Blanche de Bourbon, to leave her three days later. It was only by the entreaties of his mistress, Maria de Padilla, that he could be persuaded to return to his wife; but unable to overcome his repugnance to the poor princess, he again abandoned her a few days after, this time for ever.

The convent of La Merced owes its origin to another case of erratic passion. Donha Leonor Telles de Meneses had been torn from the arms of her first husband, João Lourenço d'Acunha, by the King of Portugal, who raised her to the throne. D'Acunha retired to Valladolid, where he was buried in the church of Santa Maria la Antigua. In the course of time Leonor's second husband also died, and she also came to Valladolid, possibly to see what had become of the first. Doubly a widow, she found consolation in the affection of a knight named Zoilo Iñiguez, by whom she had a daughter called Maria. Leonor's experience of love and matrimony led her at her death to charge her daughter's guardian, one Laserna, to dedicate the girl to religion, and to found a convent for her special accommodation. Before this could be accomplished, Maria, who believed herself to be a relation of Laserna, fell in love with his nephew, and incontinently married him. On discovering the secret of her origin, she so far complied with her mother's wish as to build a convent, in which Queen Leonor as the foundress was entombed.

About the same time, by order of Juan I., the old Alcazar, round which the town had been built, was demolished to make room for the existing convent of San Benito. The monastery of San Pablo became the residence of the court during the minority of Juan II. That king may be said to have lived here permanently, and to have confirmed Valladolid in its dignity as capital of the realm. As such it was the scene of much splendour and chivalrous display under the rule of the high-minded favourite, the great Constable Alvaro de Luna. And it was in the little Plaza del Ochavo, in the centre of the town, having run his course as a true knight and a wise statesman, that he met his fate with the dignity and composure which had distinguished him during his whole career.

The place of his execution was chosen by his enemies as precisely the scene of his greatest triumphs. He was confined during his last night in the house of his enemy, Zuñiga, where he passed the hours 'in great contrition and affliction of spirit.' 'The melancholy 2nd of June 1453 dawned,' says Don Jose Quadrado, 'and in the Plaza del Ochavo, which then formed the principal square of Valladolid, loomed a scaffold draped with black cloth, and above it a cross set with lighted tapers. On a post was fixed the spike destined to receive the severed head. The Constable was conducted to the spot by the streets of Francos, Cantarranas, and Plateria, mounted on a mule with black trappings, and preceded by a crier, whose violent denunciations drew from him only the humble words, *Más merezco* ("I deserve more"). Alighting on the side of the church of San Francisco, and mounting the scaffold with firmness, having knelt before the cross, he hesitated whether he should address the people, when he perceived among the crowd his faithful page Moreles, and Barrasa, esquire to Don Enrique. He told the latter to adjure his master not to follow the example of the king, his father, in the way of rewarding his servants; to the former he gave his signet-ring, which the youth received weeping, not a few of the bystanders weeping loudly also. "With my body they may do as they please," he said on perceiving the spike and divining its object; and baring his throat, and his hands being bound with his own girdle, he offered his head to the executioner, who a few seconds later held it up, dripping with blood, before the horror-stricken people. The body remained exposed three, and the head nine days, with a box beside it to receive alms. With these he was buried among malefactors in the hermitage of San Andrés outside the walls; but at the end of two months he was given a more decent sepulture in San Francisco, where he lay till the rehabilitation of his memory and his magnificent entombment thirty-one years later in the cathedral of Toledo.'

The feeble and ungrateful king (Juan II.) survived his favourite little more than a year, and died at the convent of San Pablo, which had been his usual abode. Valladolid remained steadily loyal to his miserable successor, Enrique IV., when scarcely another town in his dominions would harbour him. Yet, strangely enough, it was in this city, in the house of Juan Vivero (where the Audiencia now stands), that the king's sister Isabel, in defiance of his wishes, celebrated in secret, but with great ceremony, her marriage with Ferdinand of Aragon. This was on October 18, 1469—an auspicious night for Spain. But the city was too full of Enrique's partisans to afford a safe asylum to the newly-wedded pair, who immediately betook themselves to Dueñas.

Valladolid, always on the side of authority, accepted 'the Catholic Kings' on the death of Enrique, to the exclusion of Juana, whom a modern writer inexplicably calls that monarch's illegitimate daughter. She was barred from the succession on the ground that she was not his daughter at all. The vigorous but hardly beneficent rule of Ferdinand and Isabel was celebrated in 1489 by eighteen persons being burned alive in the Plaza Mayor, while a few years after the city was emptied of its Jewish inhabitants. A whole quarter left tenantless, deserted homes, and smoking human sacrifices marked the inauguration of the New Monarchy in Valladolid. Yet the city prospered, and was too busy to notice the worn-out adventurer, the Admiral of the Indies, the immortal Christopher Columbus, who died within its walls on May 20, 1506. But all their prosperity could not reconcile the sturdy citizens to the arbitrary government of

Charles v.'s regents. Valladolid threw in her lot with the Comunidad. Her sons bled in the cause of liberty beside Padilla on the fatal field of Villalar; and when the Flemish emperor proclaimed an amnesty on visiting the city in 1522, many of her townsmen found themselves among the three hundred specially excluded from its operation.

Philip II. was born here on May 21, 1527; here he was married to his first and Portuguese wife; here also she died in giving birth to his luckless son Carlos. Yet it was this native of Valladolid who reduced it to the rank of a provincial city, and in the year 1560 definitely declared Madrid to be the *unica corte*, the official capital of Spain. This measure has been variously criticised, but it is certainly difficult to perceive the advantages which the new capital possessed over the old, or over Toledo or Zaragoza. This loss of dignity was followed by a more dreadful catastrophe. Valladolid was devastated by a fire in the night of September 21, 1561, four hundred and forty houses being destroyed, though only three persons lost their lives. The silversmiths, for whom the city was renowned, saved their wares by throwing them into the wells. The conflagration was caused by the sparks blown from a fire lit by some beggars in the shadow of a wall. Possibly the citizens were reminded of those other flames so frequently kindled in their midst by the abominable Inquisition, when men and women were roasted to death in the presence and with the approval of His Catholic Majesty Philip II. The furious element was less destructive than the Holy Office.

The city was practically rebuilt by order of the despot, and as a mark of his favour he persuaded the Pope to erect it into a diocese in the last years of the sixteenth century. His successor, with a judgment of which he rarely gave proof, reinstated Valladolid in its rank of capital of the monarchy, and resided here in the palace facing San Pablo (now the Audiencia). Here Anne of Austria and Philip IV. were born. Cervantes lived here in one of the houses in the Rastro behind the Campo Grande, where he finished the first part of *Don Quixote*. His experience of the city was unfortunate. He was, together with his family, imprisoned on the charge of being implicated in a night brawl, wherein as a matter of fact he had simply played the part of Good Samaritan. His brother wits and the literati unceasingly assailed

Valladolid as unworthy the residence of the court, and after five years Philip III. was obliged, professedly because the city was unhealthy, to restore Madrid to its pre-eminence. The abandoned capital was hit very hard. Industry and commerce languished, nothing but the religious vocation flourished. The project of rendering the Duero and Pisuerga navigable for large vessels was given up, and, to crown all, the Moriscos to the number of one thousand were expelled, taking the silk industry with them. Inundations and all sorts of calamities followed in quick succession. Whatever money men earned in moribund Castile, they used to build churches and convents. The city's attachment to the Bourbon cause in the War of the Spanish Succession disposed Philip V. to transfer the court hither a second time; but the pre-eminence of Madrid was too firmly established to permit this. The French invaders, a hundred years ago, found the place ruined and stagnant. Since then Valladolid has awakened from her sleep. The opening of the North of Spain Railway, and the establishment here of the company's locomotive works, gave a great impetus to her progress, and she is now an important commercial town, the centre of the corn trade of

Castile. No Spanish city north of the Guadarrama gives such promise as Valladolid.

THE CITY

A city which was so long the capital of the monarchy—the city where Columbus died and Cervantes lived—whose streets are haunted by the immortal creature of Le Sage's genius—can be no unworthy goal for a pilgrimage. It has memories far more stirring than Madrid, which in physiognomy it rather resembles. A cold, formal town it seems at first sight, with modern-looking squares, straight streets, and severe, imposing buildings; but behind these you find the old city of Juan II. and Enrique IV., a labyrinth of tortuous lanes, gloomy palaces, and ruinous monastic houses.

The handsome Acera de Recoletos, which looks across the spacious Campo Grande—the city's principal park—leads from the triumphal Puerta del Carmen, commemorating the reign of Charles III., to the majestic Arch of Santiago. We pass through, and presently reach the Plaza Mayor, now called the Plaza de la Constitucion, the focus of the city's life.

A minor Puerta del Sol, Ford calls this regular, symmetrically planned open space, designed after the great fire of 1561 by Francisco Salamanca. The houses enclosing it are of uniform architecture, with three tiers of balconies in the three Grecian orders, capable, it is said, of accommodating 24,000 spectators. The portico is supported by massive granite columns of a bluish tinge, each a monolith. On the north side is the ungraceful Ayuntamiento (Town Hall), with weather-vanes on its towers and martial trophies surmounting the town clock. The space is as lively and gay as any in Spain. The sun shines brightly, the birds fly as freely overhead as across the innocent plains; here there is no deeper shadow than elsewhere, no abiding gloom or ghostly chill. Yet if ever a spot deserved to be called accursed it is this. Let us project ourselves back into the past, to a bright morning in May in the year 1559. The balconies have not yet been built, but stands and tiers of seats have been constructed round the Plaza. There is a grand display of bunting, and the richest draperies are hung from the crowded windows—silks and cloth of gold and silver, damasks and brocades. On a daïs are seen the little prince, Don Carlos, and his aunt the Infanta Juana. The civic dignitaries of the town are here, the craftsmen in their liveries; but making the bravest show of all are the bishop and the clergy, arrayed in full canonicals, as befits the solemn Act of Faith at which they are about to assist. The square is packed with a vast multitude—men have come from far and near to see this thing—and people are pouring down the narrow streets, an unceasing stream. All eyes are fixed on the platform in the centre of the Plaza, whereon faggots and brushwood are neatly piled round fourteen pillars, and busy varlets are bestirring themselves. A subdued murmur betokens the approach of the procession. For the alguazils who clear the way, for the horribly clad familiars of the Holy Office who stalk before, the spectators have no eyes: the gaze of those thousands is levelled on the fourteen men and women walking slowly to their awful doom. Were ever creatures so shockingly grotesque? They wear a perfectly ridiculous headgear, like an elongated nightcap, or a hat such as our grenadiers wore in days gone by; a sort of smock covers their bodies, an ugly flame-coloured garment, painted with figures of dancing and grimacing devils. You can hardly restrain a smile. I'll wager those gallants yonder are cracking some clever jokes at their expense, for the Latin is by nature a wag. We all know who they are, these wretches.

Not long before Valladolid was thrilled by the rumour that a Lutheran conventicle had been discovered here in the heart of His Most Catholic Majesty's capital. A holy woman, suspicious of her husband's orthodoxy, had followed him one day, found him in the midst of this heretical assembly, and denounced him to the Holy Office. That is the man, Juan Garcia, a goldsmith whom all the townsmen have known and dealt with this many a year. Where's his wife? somewhere in the crowd, doubtless, praying for his soul. Virtue like hers is worthy of heroines or devils. Most notable of the heretical crew is the Doctor Cazalla, one of the king's most notable preachers; but the Holy Inquisitors are no respecters of persons. They would drag you from behind the throne. The priest with the Doctor is his brother Francisco. The woman is his sister, Doña Beatriz. Burn a woman? Ay, surely. There are four more, one of them a serving-wench. That black-avised fellow is a mere Jew from Lisbon— there is little sympathy for him. Then there are four gentlemen, and—hold!—one has a gag in his mouth. It is the Bachelor, Antonio Herrer-ruelo, an obstinate fellow, who will not recede one hair's-breadth from his heretical opinions or concede one iota. The sixteen that follow interest us less. They have been reconciled with Mother Church, and for them no worse fate is reserved than the confiscation of all their goods and solitary confinement for life. Ha! one of them has fainted. It is the youthful daughter of the Marqués de Alcañias, Doña Ana Enriques. They say that one of this batch is an Englishman. Perhaps he has seen Catholics hanged, drawn, and quartered in his own land, and can forgive the Spaniard.

The learned Dominican in the pulpit reads the sentences of the Holy Tribunal of the Inquisition, and we may be sure his voice shakes with paternal tenderness when *he absolves* those who are passing into the shadow of perpetual imprisonment. As for those fourteen others—the Church has done with them, and in sorrow, not in anger, she hands them over to the secular arm.

Now who will face the flames? for even the secular arm is merciful at the eleventh hour. Thousands of eyes are strained towards the scaffold. What is passing? Cazalla is making a farewell speech. Is he obdurate? No; from mouth to mouth the rumour runs that he professes penitence, that he abjures his errors. His brothers, the women—look at their blanched faces!—mutter some such words. Their necks are encircled by the collars of the garrote—they stand on the well-laid pyre. But it is not lighted yet. Swiftly the executioner steps from one post to the other. A quiet turn of the screw, and the souls of the heretics have fled, and the flames may have their corpses.

But he with the gag, Herrerruelo? We watch him breathlessly. At all admonitions he simply shakes his head. The executioner even hesitates to fire the pile. He has his hand on the spring of the garrote. A word from the heretic, and he will be dead, unscorched, instantaneously. It is useless. Herrerruelo will not speak that word. The fire is lighted. The logs crackle and blaze. We can hardly see the victim's form. No groan nor sigh escapes him. But on his face, says one close to him, is stamped the extremest sadness that ever human being knew. Is it for yourself, Castilian of the old Roman mould? Nay, rather, I think, for your country which you see perishing beside you slowly but inevitably on the pyre of fanaticism and superstition.

It is over. The integrity of the faith of Spain has been vindicated. But the heroism of Herrerruelo soon finds imitators. His wife follows him to the flames a few years later.

Philip II. himself comes to assist at a superb act of faith which demands another holocaust. He solemnly swears to defend the faith and to enforce the decrees of its tribunal. 'And you leave me to burn?' is the bitter reproach a Veronese gentleman among the doomed men dares to address to the king. 'Ay,' says Philip, 'I would bring the wood myself to burn my own son were he a heretic.' There was thus something of the Roman spirit on both sides. The brave Italian's fortitude so inspires a fellow-sufferer that he leaps gaily into the flames, calling for wood, more wood.

The shame of the Inquisition rests not on the Spanish people. The citizens of Valladolid were kept in check on these dreadful occasions only by large bodies of troops. Torquemada, the Grand Inquisitor, dared not go forth without an armed escort of two hundred and fifty men. The Spaniards of to-day, with few exceptions, refer to the institution with expressions of abhorrence, startling even to Protestant ears. But it must be admitted that some writers more or less half-heartedly attempt a defence. Don J. M. Quadrado observes that the Holy Office saved the country from the horrors of religious wars, to which the obvious rejoinder is that the wars of religion, judged by their results, proved less disastrous to France, Germany, and Switzerland, than the policy of repression proved to Spain, and that the religious unity of other countries, such as Italy and Austria, has been preserved with comparatively little physical suasion.

We will leave the Plaza Mayor, this bright place with such gloomy memories, and see what monuments Faith has raised of a more honourable and durable kind. We cross the prettily named Place of the Golden Fountain, and the Plaza del Ochavo, where Alvaro de Luna died, and a little farther on find the Cathedral of Valladolid.

This church was begun in 1585, by order of Philip II., and replaced the old Iglesia Mayor founded by Pedro Ansúrez. The work was intrusted to Herrera, the architect of the Escorial, but his plans were never fully carried out, and the cathedral remains to-day unfinished, and also unfortunately marred by Churriguera and his disciples. The style of Herrera very eloquently expressed the temper and spirit, if not of the Spain of his day, certainly of his sovereign. The model of the church is to be seen in the muniment room. It is cruciform, the nave and transept to be flanked with aisles and chapels, the crossing to be surmounted by a dome, and a tower to be at each of the four corners. Only one of the towers was ever finished, and that collapsed in 1841; it is now being rebuilt. Street, who is very severe on all non-Gothic buildings in Spain, says that 'nothing could ever cure the hideous unsightliness of the exterior. Herrera's west front was revised by Churriguera in the eighteenth century, and cannot therefore be fairly criticised; but the side elevation remains as Herrera designed it, and is really valuable as a warning. Flying buttresses were, of course, an abomination; so in their place he erected enormous solid buttresses above the aisles to resist the thrust of the nave vault. They are shapeless blocks of masonry, projecting about forty feet from the clerestory wall, and finished with a horrid concave line at the top.'

The interior is not wanting in majesty and massiveness. Only the nave, with its aisles and chapels, has been completed. The huge piers carry bold arches, separated by a broad cornice from a plastered and panelled groined ceiling. The walls are destitute of ornament, but over the arched entrances to the chapels runs an open gallery with balustrades. The aisles have been obstructed by 'provisional chapels,' which

Herrera would have indignantly swept away; and the choir, which he intended to place behind the High Altar, is now placed so as to block the best view of the nave. The Capilla Mayor, placed in the crossing, is in bad taste, with innumerable doors and tribunes piercing its walls. One cannot but agree with the Spanish writer who says that nothing is wanting to destroy the impression of 'a grand whole,' which Herrera was especially anxious to create.

The choir stalls, mostly from the convent of San Pablo, were designed by the architect, and display some fine inlay work. The remainder are in the Gothic style, and come from the old church. The chapels contain nothing worthy of note, except a picture by Lucas Jordaens, and the tomb of Count Pedro Ansúrez, whose remains were brought here from the church he founded. A very poor effigy represents the hero, whose merits are set forth in rhymed verse.

In the sacristy is one of the finest specimens of the metal-work for which Spain has always been renowned. The solid silver monstrance, by Juan de Arfe, is $6\frac{1}{2}$ feet high, and weighs upwards of 150 lbs. It is in the shape of a temple in four stories, two of which are octagonal, and two circular. Statuettes of Adam and Eve, and a relief of the mystery of the Conception, adorn this exquisite work, for which the artificer received 44,000 reals.

Adjacent to the cathedral are some remains of the Iglesia Mayor, founded by Pedro Ansúrez, and rebuilt in the reign of St. Ferdinand. A doorway, still standing, and the various scattered pillars are in the Romanesque style, but there are also traces of Gothic work. A cloister existing at the end of the sixteenth century is described as one of the finest in Spain, containing many sculptures, all coloured, and tombs of notable people. Part of this cloister has gone to form a room called the Library, but that it still contains books I was unable to ascertain.

The Iglesia Mayor is said to have been built at the same time as the church of Santa Maria la Antigua, on the other side of the square, and both by Count Ansúrez. Comparing conflicting testimony, and the opinions of various architects, the conclusion would appear to be that the church was founded before the Count's time (for it is mentioned in documents as far back as 1088, and was in his day called the Ancient), and that the existing fabric dates mainly from the reign of Alfonso IX. (1230-44)—not from the time of the alleged restorer, Alfonso XI. Santa Maria is, beyond doubt, the most interesting church in the city. Its lofty steeple, with tiled roof and semicircular windows in all its four stages, is one of the few prominent landmarks of the wayfarer to Valladolid. The side apses are Romanesque, but the nave terminates in an apse, Gothic in style, and pierced with lancet windows. The buttresses taper off into graceful finials, with crockets and gargoyles. The main apse and transept are both pierced near the roof with an elegant openwork balustrade. The steeple is thoroughly Lombard in character.

The interior exhibits an interesting blending of the Romanesque and Gothic styles. On the outer door, defaced by a modern portico, formerly hung the knockers wrenched off the gates of the Mezquita at Cordova by the first Count Armengol. The mouldings of the arch are Romanesque, but Gothic is the beautiful groining of the interior. At the west end of the church is a gallery for the choir, with stalls and organ. In the days when this was built churches were built for the laity, and the clergy did not insist on taking up the greater part of the nave, as they did in after years. The chapel of the Counts of Cancelada contains some good paintings. The most valuable accessory is, however, the reredos by the celebrated Juan de Juni, begun in 1551 and finished in 1557. The work betrays an extraordinary degree of skill and vigour, but it is over-elaborate and in parts fantastic.

On the north this venerable church is flanked by a very beautiful Romanesque cloister of fourteen semicircular arches in three bays. The shafts, says Street, are moulded and wrought in imitation of the coupled columns of early Italian artists. This cloister, together with the steeple, makes up the most picturesque group of buildings in Valladolid, and is well worth careful preservation, if not restoration.

We will visit the University on the south side of the square another time, and will now thread our way northwards to the Plaza de San Pablo, a very interesting site. At the corner of the Calles de las Angustias and San Martin is the house where the Andalusian painter Alonso Cano is said to have killed his wife. He fled (so we are told) in consequence to his native city of Granada, where he became a prebendary of the cathedral, and executed his finest work. The church of San Martin is a very ordinary seventeenth-century structure; but it was founded soon after the resettlement of the city, and preserves its steeple, in the same style as that of Santa Maria la Antigua, and dating from about 1200. There was a baseless story that this was originally a Moorish watch-tower.

The Dominican monastery of San Pablo was founded in 1276 by Queen Violante, the rebellious consort of Alfonso XI. Maria de Molina showered favours on the community, whose friendly rivals, the Franciscans, were established in the Plaza Mayor. Later on, as we have said, Juan II. made the building his home, and died here in 1454—near to, if not in, the odour of sanctity. Here, too, the Cortes often used to sit. The present building may be considered the creation of Cardinal Juan de Torquemada (not the notorious Inquisitor), whose death took place in 1468. The façade was constructed in the latter part of the fifteenth century, and restored in the seventeenth and nineteenth centuries; it is a debased late-Gothic style, the main object of the architects being evidently to multiply evidences of their skill. In this they succeeded, for no one can question the merit of the execution. The riotous exuberance of the decoration renders a description difficult. The doorway is placed within an arch of a curious waved line. On either side are shown saints of the order, standing on pedestals, with pinnacle-like canopies above them. Above the arch is an indifferent relief of the Coronation of the Blessed Virgin, attended by Cardinal Torquemada with his patron saints, the Baptist and the Evangelist. All this part of the decoration is enclosed within an ugly flattened arch. Above is the figure of Christ Enthroned, and on each side of Him a trefoil arch containing the figures of the Four Evangelists. These arches frame windows with exquisite traceries, such as fill the circular window above the Christ. The upper part of the façade is in three stages, each filled with figures of saints and heraldic devices. 'Every vacant space,' says Street, 'seems to have a couple of angels holding coats-of-arms, so that it is impossible not to feel that the sculptor and the founder must have had some idea of heaven as peopled by none with less than a proper number of quarterings on their shields, or without claim to the possession of *Sangre Azul*.' The arms displayed on the lower part of the façade are not, however, those of Torquemada, but of the Duke of Lerma, the favourite of Philip III., by whom the church was restored. Here he celebrated his first Mass in the year 1618, having sought refuge in the church from the cares of state, or the disappointments of a courtier's life;

and here, too, he was ultimately buried. The church was plundered and dismantled by the French during the Peninsular War, and the interior is now inaccessible to visitors.

On the other side of the Plazuela is the palace built by Lerma on the site of the house where Don Carlos was born, and sold by him to Philip III. for thirty-seven million maravedis. The façade is simple, not undignified, and adorned with the royal arms over the doorway. The patio, or inner quadrangle, is decorated with busts of the Roman emperors and the arms of the old provinces of Spain. Here, says Ford, Napoleon took up his quarters on that memorable visit to Spain which at once altered the complexion of affairs. The building is now the Audiencia, or Law Court.

Philip II. was born in the house at the corner of the square and the Calle Cadesa de San Gregorio, and baptized in the church of San Pablo. Except for its associations, the house is uninteresting.

Next to San Pablo is the Colegio San Gregorio, built by Alonso de Burgos, Isabel the Catholic's Confessor, in remembrance of his student days at the former establishment. The work, elaborate as it is, occupied only eight years—1488 to 1496.

The architect, Matias Carpintero, for some unknown reason committed suicide before its completion in 1490. The façade of the main entrance resembles that of the older foundation. The design displays more originality, but the execution is by no means as good. The lintel and jambs of the square doorway are decorated by a relieved pattern of fleur-de-lys, and enclosed within an arched canopy of fanciful outline. On either side of the doorway are statues of wild men—possibly an allusion to the discovery of America—and over the lintel a relief represents the founder kneeling before the patron saint. From the canopy, twisted tapering pillars soar upwards and divide the upper stage into three parts. The middle one is occupied by the relief of a pomegranate tree springing from a basin, and sheltering children and birds among its branches; it supports the coat-of-arms of Ferdinand and Isabel. The lateral divisions contain figures supporting escutcheons, the whole being 'even more extremely heraldic in its decorations' than San Pablo. The open-work, cusping at the top, looks as if made of coarse wicker-work, and is happily fast disappearing under the corrosive effects of frost and rain. The interior of San Gregorio wearies the eye with its excess of heraldic decoration. The inner court, notwithstanding, is noble and spacious, with a double gallery of six arches on each side springing from spirally-fluted columns. The fleur-de-lys appear on the arms of the founder; the yoke and sheaf of arrows are the well-known devices of the Catholic kings. The chapel was stripped by the French of all of value that it contained, including the sepulchral effigy of Alonso de Burgos. The college is now one of the municipal buildings.

The secularised church and convent of San Benito on the west side of the town were founded by Juan I. on the site of the old Alcazar, in reparation for a Benedictine house destroyed by his father. The actual fabric was commenced in 1453, and hardly completed three centuries later. The plan of the church reminds one of Santa Maria la Antigua. The interior is lofty and impressive. There are two choirs—one in the western gallery, and the other, as usual in Spain, in the middle of the church, and enclosed by brick walls. The church was very strongly built, and is, appropriately enough, occupied by the military.

In the church of La Magdalena is buried Bishop Pedro de la Gasca, who recovered Peru for the monarchy from the clutches of Pizarro.

His tomb in the centre of the transept was chiselled by Esteban Jordán in 1577.

The other churches of Valladolid hardly repay a visit. We may now turn our attention to the University, close to the Antigua Church. Founded in the eleventh century, this institution rose into importance only on the decline of the University of Salamanca. The statues of its patrons—Alfonso VIII., Alfonso XI., Juan I., and Enrique III.—surmount the grotesque and extravagant façade, which is in the worst baroque or Churrigueresque style. Older and more interesting are the English and Scots Colleges. The former was founded by Sir Francis Englefield in 1590 or thereabouts, for the education of young Englishmen for the Catholic priesthood. The Scots College is an analogous institution, founded by Colonel Sempill at Madrid in 1627, and transferred hither in 1771. The Irish College is at Salamanca. Both seminaries are still resorted to, to some extent, by youths from the United Kingdom, though a novitiate in Valladolid might not seem an adequate training for parochial work in English cities or Highland glens.

Sculpture is the art that has been least cultivated in Spain. Exceptional interest attaches, therefore, to the Museum of Valladolid, which contains a valuable collection of the works of native sculptors, or rather carvers. The building itself is the old College of Santa Cruz, built in 1486 by the famous Enrique de Egas, and intended by the founder, Cardinal Mendoza (*el tercer Rey*) to harbour impoverished genius. The exterior is surmounted by a balustrade, and strengthened with buttresses tapering into pinnacles. The principal façade is a fine example of Plateresque work, with much that is Gothic about the detail. The coats-of-arms of the Catholic kings and of the founder appear, of course, in the decoration, and the cardinal is shown adoring the cross upheld by St. Helen. The inner court is surrounded by a triple tier of galleries, with semicircular arches, octagonal pillars, and elegant balustrades.

Within these walls have been collected treasures from the demolished, dismantled, and disused churches, convents, and palaces of the city, many of the objects now here having been removed from their original positions by the French and left behind them in the hurry of flight. Here we find the retablo executed between 1526 and 1532 for the church of San Benito by Alonso Berruguete. Street, who disliked all the works of the Renaissance, denounced this altarpiece in unmeasured terms; but no impartial critic can deny the beauty of certain of the figures, notably those of Abraham and St. Sebastian. In the museum may also be seen the choir stalls from the same church, carved by the master in 1528—ten years before he designed the *silleria* of Toledo. The work displays marvellous imagination and great delicacy in the execution.

The genius of Juan de Juni, who was living at Valladolid in 1570, is best represented by his wooden statue of the Dead Christ, from the convent of San Francisco. So ghastly is the realism of this figure, that looking at the rigid limbs—more like those of a gladiator than of the Crucified—we feel that corruption is about to take place, and avert our eyes in horror. One is tempted to hold one's nose, as Murillo is said to have done while contemplating a canvas by Valdes Leal. Not less vigorous and infinitely more attractive is the noble statue of St. Bruno by the same sculptor.

Gregorio Hernandez was the last of the trio of carver-sculptors who lived and worked at Valladolid. He was an indefatigable and prolific worker, and never doubted that the sole mission of art was to serve the purposes of religion. He died in 1636, in Juni's old house, at No. 37 Calle de San Luis. He is well represented in this museum. St. Teresa is perhaps his best work, but shows his want of vigour as compared with his two predecessors. It was Hernandez who unfortunately set the example of draping statues with nets and fabrics, since followed with such unhappy results.

Few artists on canvas, or in stone or wood, have so well expressed the evil passions of the mob as the unknown sculptor of Christ bearing the Cross. The multitude is composed, of course, of local types—of those ferocious bravos and audacious picaros who abounded in Spain at that time, and whose ugliest characteristics are here caught and rendered with astonishing realism. A different genius is exemplified by the beautiful statues in bronze gilt of the Duke and Duchess of Lerma, which once decorated their tombs at San Pablo. They were begun by an Italian, Pompeio Leoni, but completed, it is believed, by another hand.

The pictures in the museum are not of great importance. The Assumption and two other works by Rubens are in bad condition, and almost surpassed in interest by some pleasing productions of the modern Spanish school.

Not far from the museum is the house where Columbus died (No. 7 Cristobal Colon). He came hither on his return from his last voyage in 1504, and languished here, absolutely neglected by the cold-hearted Ferdinand, for eighteen months. From Philip and Joanna he hoped to obtain a fuller recognition of his services, and upon their landing in Spain he sent them the assurance of his homage and respect. Philip acknowledged this in a generous and kindly spirit—an act which, together with his oft-expressed disapprobation of the Inquisition, should be remembered to the handsome Burgundian's credit. But on the 21st May 1506, Columbus went on a longer voyage than any he had made to the Indies—to the undiscovered country whence no traveller returns. He left two sons—Hernando, who, like his father, lies in the cathedral of Seville, and Diego, the ancestor of the present Duke of Veragua.

The house of Cervantes, of which I have already spoken in the historical chapter, is in the Calle de Miguel Iscar, leading from the Acero de Recoletos to the Mercado.

Interesting old houses are not uncommon in Valladolid. Besides those already mentioned are the Casas del Cordon and de los Duendes, built in part in the reign of Juan II.; the palace of Fabio Neli, the great patron of art and letters in Valladolid, with its classical doorway; the archiepiscopal palace, once the residence of the Marquises of Villasante; and the house of the unfortunate Calderon, minister of Philip III., in the Calle de Teresa Gil. Berruguete's workshop may be seen near the convent (now barracks) of San Benito.

These memorials of the city's golden age having been inspected, you may ruminate on its past and future (for Valladolid *has* a future) in the beautiful shaded promenades by the Pisuerga or beneath the trees of the Magdalena park; and thus refreshed may possibly be ready to investigate the archives of the kingdom at Simancas, seven miles away. Considerable time and patience will, however, be required, since the collection consists of upwards of thirty-three millions of documents, arranged in eighty thousand bundles.

II

OVIEDO

THE province of Asturias is, for all men of Spanish blood, holy ground. Its fastnesses sheltered the last little remnant of the nation which refused to bow before the foreign yoke, its mountains proved an impregnable bulwark against the invader. At Covadonga, Spain, beaten to her knees, with broken sword and buckler, struck back wildly, despairingly. Her adversary recoiled; in that instant she recovered her breath, and, rising to her feet, pressed him steadily, stealthily, irresistibly backwards. Asturias was not the cradle, but the asylum of the Spanish nation. Here, to use familiar expressions, she found salvation in the last ditch; she was saved at the eleventh hour.

How dreadful was the peril of the nation we may understand when we read that the coast of Asturias itself was overrun by the Moors, and that a Muslim governor ruled at Gijon. Only a few glens in the wild Cantabrian mountains can boast a soil never profaned by the tread of the infidel. Oviedo can claim no such distinction. The ground on which she stands was, beyond all doubt, within the Moorish dominions. And she was not, as it is a very common error to suppose, the first capital of the reborn monarchy. It was at Cangas de Onis that Pelayo held his primitive court, and to Pravia, nearer the ocean, that Silo transferred the seat of government. Not till the reign of Alfonso the Chaste (791-842) did Oviedo become the capital of the infant monarchy.

The town was younger even than the kingdom. It sprang up round a monastery founded by King Froila I. on the spot where in 760 the Abbot Fromistano had dedicated a humble church to St. Vincent. Before the monastery was built, the first stones were laid of the famous basilicas of the Salvador and of Saints Julian and Basilissa. Alfonso was born here, and partly out of affection for his native place, partly perhaps from an aversion to the capital of his enemy, Mauregato, he established his court here, beside the churches he loved. He girded the town with walls, and raised the bishop to the rank of primate of his dominions. Sovereign of two of the smaller provinces of Spain, he is said to have been emulous of the splendour of his contemporary Charlemagne. He endeavoured to restore the state of the old Gothic court. He revived the laws, the customs, and the ritual of his ancestors, and imported precious woods and marbles from afar for the embellishment of his little capital. His successors imitated not only the ceremonial and luxury of the Byzantine Emperors, but also their intriguing and methods of punishment. Putting out the eyes was as popular a means of ridding oneself of an opponent at Oviedo as at Constantinople. Alfonso el Magno avenged himself in this way on his four brothers, Veremundo, Nuño, Odoario, and Froila, whom he detected conspiring against him. Veremundo, notwithstanding, escaped to Astorga, where the inhabitants espoused his cause and defended him against his brother. Another conspiracy proved more successful, and Alfonso was driven from the throne by his own son. One day the dethroned sovereign presented himself before his successor and craved a boon. It was to lead the Asturian hosts once more against the infidels. The request was granted, and victory, as it had always done, attended the old king's banners. And he had no sooner laid aside his arms, than, crowned with laurels in place of a diadem, he passed away at Zamora, December 20, 910.

The dominions of Alfonso were dismembered at his abdication, and Oviedo for the brief space of twenty years remained the capital of the kingdom of Asturias alone. Ramiro II. reunited the monarchy, and at the same time transferred the capital to Leon. Oviedo became again the temporary seat of government, when Al Mansûr's ever-victorious host swept over Spain, submerging all the Christian conquests, and breaking only against the impenetrable barrier of the Asturias. Leon was not restored to its rank till the reign of Alfonso V. (999-1027). This second period of residence of the kings at Oviedo was marked by the miraculous intervention of Heaven on behalf of an innocent man—if the chroniclers may be credited. Ataulfo, Bishop of Santiago, was accused of enormous crimes, and, having been summoned to the court, was condemned on insufficient evidence by Veremundo II. to be exposed to the fury of a wild bull. The prelate, strong in the knowledge of his innocence, celebrated Mass, and presented himself in the arena clad in his pontifical vestments. The furious animal entered, and lo! at once prostrated himself before the devoted man, offering his head and horns to be caressed. Nay, more, he threatened the spectators with his fury. Amid the plaudits of all, the holy bishop withdrew, and retired to a church in the valley of the Pravia, where he died in the odour of sanctity. Oviedo was known as the city of the bishops, as it was the residence of a great many prelates whose Sees were *in partibus infidelium*—that is to say, had passed under the control of the Moors.

The history of the city, and indeed of the province, from the tenth century onwards, is of scant interest. Asturias was erected by Alfonso VII. in 1153 for a brief space into an independent kingdom in favour of the Infanta Urraca, his natural daughter by a lady of the province; but on her death it was reunited to the monarchy of Castile and Leon. Oviedo was too remote from the scene of the long campaign against the Muslims and from the later seats of government to take any prominent part in the nation's affairs. But it did not escape the assaults of the French in the Peninsular War. The town was remorselessly sacked by General Bonnet, in spite of a resistance not unworthy of the posterity of Pelayo's unconquerable warriors.

A quiet, clean city, swept unceasingly by wind

and rain, Oviedo at first sight recalls but faintly its glorious past. Yet when we look carefully about us, we find that time has been kind to those early sanctuaries which were the cause of the town's existence, and which have merited for it the title of 'the holy.' Approaching more as a pilgrim than a critic, in no sceptical frame of mind, you will find few places in Spain more deeply interesting. And though it is neither the oldest nor the most interesting architecturally of the local monuments, your steps will turn at once to the Cámara Santa, attached to the cathedral— the Palladium of Spain.

In the seventh century (so runs the legend) when the hosts of Khosru threatened the Holy Land, an ark or coffer, worked by the disciples of the Apostles and full of relics of ineffable sanctity, was conveyed by pious hands to Egypt. Thence it was transported to Cartagena, thence to Toledo; and when that city in its turn was menaced by the ever-advancing Saracen, it was taken by King Pelayo to the cave of Monsagro, ten miles from Oviedo. When the chaste king and his architect, Tioda, re-erected the basilica of San Salvador, founded by Froila, in the year 802, a chapel dedicated to San Miguel, and now called the Cámara Santa, was built expressly to receive this venerated reliquary.

This sanctuary is now approached from the south side of the cathedral by a flight of twenty-two steps, built in the sixteenth century. We reach first the chapel, or ante-cámara, restored if not entirely constructed in the reign of Alfonso VI. (1072-1109), and representing the highest pitch of development reached at that time by Romanesque art in Spain. The roof is groined, and supported on each side by six columns built into the wall. Each column consists of two pilasters, rising from high pedestal bases, and supporting the statues of two Apostles. These figures are expressive, though rude, and the draperies are graceful and natural. At their feet are fantastic animals. The capitals of the columns are richly and beautifully carved with foliage, and with compositions representing scenes from the life of the Saviour and combats between men and lions. The capitals of the small pillars at the corners of the pedestals are also curious and delicately carved. Over the door are three heads in relief, of Christ, the Virgin, and St. John, early Romanesque work once painted and then disfigured by whitewash. The pavement of hard *argamasa*, or tessellated work, resembles, as Ford remarks, Norman-Byzantine works in Sicily. Beneath is a crypt, or lower chapel, dedicated to St. Leocadia.

At the far end of the Ante-cámara is the Relicario, the sanctuary actually constructed by Alfonso the Chaste. It measures about 19½ by 17 feet, and consists of a single low vault with traces of paintings, and lighted by a little window in the arch spanning the entrance.

Enclosed within a railing is the *Arca*, a chest of oak, 7½ feet long by 3¾ broad, and thinly plated with silver. A Latin inscription of four lines on the lid goes to prove that this was the work, not of Alfonso the Chaste, but of Alfonso VI., a conclusion warranted also by the Arabic inscription in Kufic characters, in praise of the Most High, running round the chest—a form of decoration not introduced into Christian work till after the fall of Toledo. On one face of the ark are reliefs of the Twelve Apostles within niches, with the Four Evangelists at the angles, and the figure of Christ, supported by angels, in the middle. On one side are reliefs of the Nativity, Adoration of the Shepherds, and the Flight into Egypt; on the other the Revolt of Satan, the Ascension, and the Apostles. The subject of the reliefs on the cover is the Crucifixion.

What this ark contains is a matter for pious speculation. It is reckoned rash and impious to attempt to solve the mystery; and it is related that when Bishop Sandoval y Rojas, after much prayer and fasting, placed the key in the lock, he experienced such horror that his hair rose erect and knocked off his mitre! It is extraordinary that Bonnet's soldiers did not attempt to solve the mystery.

On the cover of the Arca are placed smaller reliquaries, beautiful specimens of silversmith's work, which some may think of more interest than their contents. These, according to tradition, are the following: two thorns from Christ's crown, and one of the deniers for which he was sold; a piece of St. Bartholomew's skin; some drops of blood which exuded from a crucifix profaned by the Jews; a fragment of the rod of Moses; one of St. Peter's sandals; a fragment of the True Cross; and certain ivory tablets dated 1162.

Other precious relics are exhibited in the chamber, among them the winding-sheet of the Saviour, in a superb box of gold and blue enamel. The Cruz de la Victoria was carved of plain oak and carried as a standard by Pelayo at Covadonga; it is now encrusted with gold and brilliant enamels—work executed, as the inscription records, at Gauzon, near Oviedo, in the year 908. Another cross, styled the Cruz de los Angeles, dates from the times of Alfonso the Chaste, for whom it was made, it is said, by two angels disguised as goldsmiths. This precious relic is in the shape of a Maltese cross, is set with gems *en cabochon*, and encrusted with gilt filigree-work. In the centre is set a precious ruby. On the arms is inscribed the date of the making (808 A.D.) and an anathema on whomsoever should steal it. It is certainly remarkable that this inscription should contain nothing about the supernatural workmanship of the cross!

The cathedral built by Tioda by order of Alfonso the Chaste was pulled down in the twelfth century. The foundation of the existing edifice may be attributed to Bishop Gutierre de Toledo, who flourished about 1390. The work was continued zealously by his successors, but was not altogether completed till the sixteenth century was half gone. The west front is flanked by towers, only one of which, as so often happens in Spain, has been raised above the general roof-level. The southern tower is of singular dignity and beauty. It rises to the height of 224 feet, and is divided into five stages, of which three are above the level of the aisles. The massive piers on which the structure rests are continued upwards in the form of buttresses along the corners, and are fluted, moulded, and enriched with canopies, crockets, and ornaments of the most elaborate and at the same time tasteful character. The windows are of three lights, with good traceries, above the archivolts appearing a kind of trefoil ornament. The third stage is girt by a beautiful parapet. The fourth stage is rather Renaissance than Gothic in treatment. It is flanked by tapering finials, and constitutes the belfry. Here is hung the bell named after King Vamba, which dates from 1219. On the topmost stage rises the graceful steeple, thickly encrusted with crockets, and flanked by pinnacles which seem to be a reproduction of it in miniature. No more beautiful church steeple than this is to be seen in Spain, or indeed in Europe. Repeated restorations, notably in 1521 and 1728, have fortunately left its fairy-like symmetry unimpaired.

The tower, however, unquestionably dwarfs the rest of the front, which is composed of a fine portico of three arches, the middle one being the highest. This central porch is flanked by statues of Alfonso the Chaste and King Froila. Despite these, and the canopied niches in the buttresses, the whole front presents a bare and forbidding aspect, not devoid, it must be conceded, of majesty. The portico was evidently only intended to be the base of the towers, of which, as we have seen, one only has been erected.

The interior is harmonious and pleasing. The nave is about twice the height of the aisles, with which it communicates through pointed arches. The piers are lightly fluted and encircled by simple fillets of foliage. Above the arches runs a gallery with a graceful balustrade, and pointed openings divided by mullions and containing good traceries. The clerestory windows are tall and of six lights, the mullions being bent so as to form tracery. On the south side they are filled with good stained glass; the northern windows are filled up. The transepts are spacious and lighted by wheel windows. There is no lantern over the crossing.

The chancel occupies a pentagonal apse at the east end of the nave, lit with five stained-glass windows. The retablo, dating from 1440, but since restored, is indifferent. The subjects of the reliefs are taken from the life of Christ.

Near the High Altar are the tombs of various bishops, and a fine kneeling effigy of Bishop del Villar, who is buried at Segovia. The pulpits are of gilt iron. In the Renaissance chapels behind the chancel is the tomb of Bishop Gutierre.

In the transept is a rudely sculptured figure of Christ, believed to date from the twelfth century. The shells sculptured on the capital of the pillar, against which it stands, refer to the pilgrims who frequented this famous shrine.

The choir stalls are richly carved with caprices and scenes, 'ill according,' remarks a Spanish writer, 'with the sanctity of the place.' But the backs of the lower seats bear representations of Biblical characters, which, like the canopies above, are exquisitely carved. The organs are Churrigueresque, and the gorgeous Gothic trascoro is in hardly better taste. The chapels date mostly from the seventeenth and eighteenth centuries, and contain nothing of interest, except the alleged body of St. Eulalia of Merida.

Communicating with the north transept is the Capilla del Rey Casto. This chapel, founded by Alfonso the Chaste, was entirely rebuilt in the eighteenth century by a bishop named Melaz in the worst baroque style. This was the pantheon of the early kings of Asturias, and some tombs, probably containing their remains, are certainly here; but the inscriptions are merely the result of guess-work. Only one sarcophagus can be identified, and that, it appears from the inscription, is the resting-place of one Ithacus. Who this personage was, and what he had done to merit sepulture in the royal vault, are riddles to which history supplies no answer.

The cloister, begun in the fourteenth and finished in the fifteenth century, is in good Gothic style. The pointed arches looking on the court are divided by four or five slender shafts, which support elegant tracery. Among the statues that of Alfonso XI. is the best preserved. The capitals and corbels are curiously and richly carved with such subjects as King Favila hunting the bear, the duel of Froila, and what Mr. O'Shea very rightly calls 'a series of comical pictorial reviews of the times.' There are many tombs in the cloister, belonging to various epochs, mostly earlier than the fourteenth century. They are of all styles, but Don J. M. Quadrado points out that the epitaphs are almost uniform in style. The famous Bishop Pelayo's tomb (died 1153) is here.

The chapter-house is a fine specimen of thirteenth-century architecture. The archives adjoining contain some documents and codices of the greatest value. Here is preserved the *Libro Gotico* of the twelfth century, a beautifully illuminated manuscript, throwing light on the costumes and customs of that day.

The other churches founded by Alfonso the Chaste and his predecessors in the town itself have either been demolished or so often restored, rebuilt, and renovated, that they cannot be considered worth a visit. The earliest foundation of all, San Vicente, was modernised in 1592, and is interesting as containing the bones of the Abbot Feijoo, a man greatly esteemed by his contemporaries for his learning and sanctity (died 1764).

The Gothic church of San Francisco, now attached to a hospital, was founded by Fray Pedro, a companion of the great Francis of Assisi himself. This is the burying-place of the great family of Quirós, which claimed, in a not very reverent distich, to rank in point of dignity and antiquity next to the Divinity ('Después de Dios, la casa de Quirós'). In the chancel lies Gonzalo Bernaldo de Quirós the Older, the youthful friend of Enrique of Trastamara, who died, wearing the religious habit, in 1575. Within a sepulchre upheld by lions which bear escutcheons crossed by the bar sinister, are the ashes of another Gonzalo Bernaldo, a distinguished illegitimate scion of the house. He is shown clad in armour, and at his feet a dog—symbolical, possibly, of the fidelity and tenacity with which he watched over the interests of his family during the minority of its chiefs. Close by is the vault of the house of Valdecarzana; a modern inscription informs us that during the interment of one of that family, a live cow must be present in the church—why or wherefore not being stated.

The church of Santa Maria de la Vega, outside the town, was the chapel of a Benedictine nunnery founded by Gontroda, mistress of Alfonso VII., who took the veil here in 1154. She was joined in her retirement, it is believed, by her daughter Urraca, sometime Queen of Navarre, and afterwards of Asturias. A century later another interesting penitent sought an asylum here: Doña Sancha Alvarez, mistress of the greatest noble in Spain, Rodrigo Alvarez de Asturias. The two ladies' tombs lie close together. The sarcophagus of Gontroda is adorned with Romanesque reliefs of birds, and of hounds chasing deer, in curiously crude and conventional attitudes; Sancha's tomb shows Gothic influence, and is sculptured in low relief. The epitaphs extol the virtues and amiability of the departed ladies.

The two most interesting monuments in the district are the ancient churches of Santa Maria de Naranco and San Miguel de Lino, both outside the walls. The former was rebuilt by Ramiro I., and is, therefore, well over a thousand years old. Attached to it were a palace and baths, every trace of which has long since disappeared. The architecture presents curious local peculiarities. The church is situated on a slope, and is composed of a single nave resting on a crypt or substructure. The only entrance is by a porch on the north side, which is on the level of the nave and approached by steps. The whole exterior is severe and simple, strong buttresses running up the walls to the sloping roof. In the west front three stages may be distinguished: the lowest is formed by the substructure entered in the middle by a round arch; above this the nave terminates in a portico of three round arches, which spring from four palm-like pillars with Corinthian capitals; in the middle of the third stage is a window of three lights, also round arched. The interior has remained practically unchanged since Ramiro's day. The chancel and choir occupy opposite ends of the nave, and are raised by one and three steps respectively above the level of the flooring. Both are shut off by three round arches, the middle one being higher than the others; and an arcade of closed arches runs along the side-walls of the nave. These arches are rudely constructed, and rest upon, rather than spring from, octagonal capitals, quaintly carved with figures of priests and lions. The columns are composed each of four engaged shafts, of the same pattern as those of the western portico. The ribs of the waggon-vaulted ceiling spring from corbels, beneath which are reliefs representing the two orders of society in Asturias in the ninth century—knights engaged in combat, and toilers carrying loads. Under these again are circular medallions, filled with conventional foliage, and having in the centre reliefs of lions and birds. The church was probably intended to be open at both ends, as it is now, that the congregation assembled on the hillside might be able to assist in divine worship. It is one of the most valuable architectural monuments of Spain.

The little basilica of San Miguel de Lino was

built near Santa Maria by King Ramiro about the year 850. The name was originally *de ligno*, *i.e.* of the wood, and was derived quite possibly from a fragment of the True Cross preserved here. Here we have a cruciform church in miniature, with transepts, lantern, and apsidal chapels, of a height which seems out of proportion to their other reduced dimensions. The apsidal chapels formed a semicircle at the foundation, but have been squared off since. The roofs are tiled and pitched. The buttresses resemble those of the Naranco church. The walls are pierced, here and there, with windows of three lights, with round arches, columns spirally fluted, and columns cut into leaves; above these is an elaborate geometrical tracery, suggestive of Moorish influence. The jambs of the round-arched western porch are rudely carved with curious groups. One of these is irresistibly grotesque. A man is shown balancing himself with his hands on the top of a pole and his legs in the air, exactly like the familiar monkey on a stick of our childhood; with head downwards, he grins into the jaws of a lion, which stands on its hind legs agape with surprise or indignation. Behind the gymnast another man appears to be indulging in some sort of dumb-bell exercise. This amazing composition is averred by some authorities to represent the martyrdom of a saint! The floral designs which border it are skilfully, even delicately, executed.

The chancel is on a lower level than the nave, which is reached on each side by a flight of steps, in a chapel projecting from the transept. The lantern has one of the earliest attempts at a domed roof, now unfortunately concealed by a later flat ceiling. The columns and arches are Byzantine in style, and the capitals carved with rosettes in medallions and strapwork. The nave is waggon vaulted and lower than the transept.

The modern buildings of Oviedo present few features of interest. The old walls have almost entirely disappeared, and few of the palaces or noblemen's houses date further back than the seventeenth century. The University, founded in 1608 by the executors of Archbishop de Valdés, is a dignified building in the classical style—such as one might see in any fair-sized town in southern Europe. The Ayuntamiento, uninteresting in itself, contains a charter granted by the sixth and confirmed by the seventh

Alfonso. Those who have had the opportunity of studying it say that it illustrates the transition from Latin to Spanish—just as the history of Oviedo illustrates the development of the Goth into the Spaniard.

III

SEGOVIA

THE ancient and beautiful city of Segovia occupies one of those sites which men would have chosen for the building of towns as soon as towns ever came to be built. We may therefore be sure that the roots of the city's life lie very far back in the past—an assurance confirmed by the name, which bespeaks an Iberian origin. Mediæval writers mentioned this as among the towns built by the fabulous King Hispan, whose name, with those of his relatives, Iberia and Pyrrhus, is always introduced to explain a mystery or to adorn a tale. To the Romans the place was known as Segobriga; and that it was a flourishing and important colony the great aqueduct, the most famous of its monuments, remains to this day to attest. We may assume the town under the Roman yoke was happy, for it had no history—at least, nothing of it has reached us. There were bishops on these barren heights in early times, for they are referred to by name as attending councils at Toledo in the sixth and seventh centuries. At the time of the Mohammedan conquest, a hermit called Fruto rallied the Christians in the fastnesses of the mountains and kept alive in them the Christian faith and traditions. This holy person was the brother of the martyrs Valentin and Engracia, whom the Moors put to death. This the hardened infidels did, the chroniclers assure us, in spite of miracles which might have converted Mohammed himself; for the Segovian saints cleft mountains asunder with the stroke of a knife, and produced fountains from the solid rock with the touch of a wand; while a mare, to whom the Eucharist had been offered as food, dropped on her knees in adoration. It is clear that in after years the Christians of Segovia enjoyed the liberty of worship that the Muslims of Spain everywhere conceded to their subjects; for we hear of a bishop, Ildered, governing his flock here in the year 940. In the following century it was included within the dominions of the Amir of Toledo, and on the downfall of that monarchy was annexed to the growing kingdom of Castile.

Like Salamanca and Avila, Segovia was repeopled at the instance of Count Raymond of Burgundy, chiefly by Gallegos from the north-west. It received its first charter from Alfonso VI. in 1108. Thereafter its citizens were always to be found in the fighting line. Tradition avers that Madrid was recovered from the Moors by the Segovians; and their chiefs on that glorious occasion were Dia Sanz and Fernán Garcia, whose descendants for many years after divided the government of the city between them. But the chronicles register a very black stain on the city's fame: the assassination by the townsfolk of Alvar Fañez, the illustrious brother-in-arms of Alfonso VI., at Easter, 1114. Four years later, the Segovians took the side of Alfonso VII. against his mother, Queen Urraca, and were rewarded by the reconstitution of their town into a bishopric.

The history of Segovia differs little from that of other Castilian towns. Its citizens shared the glories and the hardships of the ceaseless campaigns against the Moors, and did not hold aloof from the equally numerous civil wars that distracted the kingdom. In 1295 they refused submission to the young king, Fernando IV., and his mother, Maria de Molina. The brave queen forced her way into the town, and found the gates shut behind her. Undismayed, she harangued the stubborn townsmen. 'Open your gates,' she cried, 'and I will go with my son to more grateful and obedient towns; where vassals are less easily deceived by intriguers, and where mother and son are not separated!' The people were moved by her reproaches, and, admitting the king, escorted both in triumph to the Alcazar.

The minority of Alfonso XI. (1320) was attended by sanguinary disorders in the streets of Segovia. Every church and house became a fortress, and the rival factions stormed and laid siege to each other's strongholds within the narrow compass of the city walls. In 1368 the nobility held the Alcazar for Enrique of Trastamara, whilst the commons held the town for Pedro the Cruel; but the Gracious King, after the death of his half-brother at Montiel, visited Segovia and won all hearts. A hundred years later the town was distinguished by its loyalty to the wretched Enrique IV., who here betrayed his own daughter, Juana, by a reconciliation with his sister, Isabel. Not content with this, he appeared in the streets, leading by the bridle the palfrey of the woman who denied his own child's legitimacy.

The townsfolk, at the beginning of the reign of Charles V., threw in their lot with the Comuneros; but the Alcazar throughout the rising was held by the royal forces. The

King-Emperor and his successor, like their predecessors, frequently sojourned in the old palace-fortress. Later on, it was often used as a state prison. The famous Ripperdá, the Dutch adventurer, passed a portion of his captivity here; and the Marquis of Ayamonte was confined here prior to his execution in 1648. The establishment of the court permanently at Madrid, and the building of La Granja by Philip V. in 1721, diminished the importance of Segovia as a royal residence. In few countries have the larger provincial towns loomed more conspicuously in the past than in Spain, and in few are they nowadays more decayed and bloodless. Segovia remains, as Antonio Gallenga described it, 'an unmatched picture of the Middle Ages. You read its history on the old city walls with their eighty-three towers; in the domes and belfries of its churches; in the bare and blank ruins of its deserted monasteries; in the battlemented towers of its noble mansions.'

The town stands high and bravely on the mountains, its flanks washed by two clear streams, Eresma and Clamores. The towers and domes rise sharply against the clear sky, high above the surrounding hills; an island of the air Segovia seems as you catch sight of her from the dusty plains of Old Castile. Even as clouds in their fantastic formations take the semblance of far-away cities, so at certain hours from afar off you might take this to be just such a cloud-town. And when you draw nearer you find the valleys are cool and green, and that the tall trees flourish here and do not wither as in the plains round Burgos and Valladolid.

Coming from La Granja, the first you see of Segovia's wonders is fittingly by far the oldest. The aqueduct dates, it is believed, from Trajan's reign, and is the most considerable of the Roman remains of Spain. In the Middle Ages, like most other classical works, it was attributed to diabolical agency, and is still often called El Puente del Diablo. Beginning at the Fuente Fria in the Sierra Guadarrama, ten miles away, with many zigzags it passes over hill and dale, and at last spans the deep valley before the city, and is carried across the streets to the Alcazar. It is built of granite with black veins, hewn in great blocks, which are pieced together without mortar or clamps. Every block is visible on one side or another. For the distance of nine hundred yards the aqueduct is carried on one hundred and nineteen arches, varying in height from twenty-three to ninety-four feet. For a third of this length the arches are in two tiers. The work is devoid of ornamentation, except for the remains of a cornice. All is not Roman work. The aqueduct was partially demolished in the eleventh century during a siege by the Moors, and when Queen Isabel the Catholic determined to restore it, thirty-six arches between the convents of La Concepcion and San Francisco had fallen in. The restoration of these was intrusted, on the recommendation of the Prior of El Parral, to a young monk of that house, named Fray Juan Escovedo, who performed his difficult task with remarkable skill. Indeed, it is not easy to distinguish the Spaniard's work from the Roman's. Escovedo died in 1489. The only reward he received for his labours was the timber of the scaffoldings.

Some of the arches have been for centuries embedded in the city walls. The work, though severe and imposing, is not perhaps equal to the Pont de Gard, or even to certain other Roman remains in Spain. Yet nothing could be more curious, or, in a sense, more picturesque, than the views of the quaint old houses framed by its arches, or grander than these as seen from San Juan, or towering above the Plaza Mayor. Their height is, of course, magnified by the hovels clustering at their bases, in comparison with which the aqueduct appears rather the work of Cyclopes than of men. And through these arches, as through a gate of triumph, we pass into the mediæval city.

Yet this is not the only monument of classical antiquity in Segovia. The rude figure of Hercules about to slay the Erymanthine Boar was discovered in the interior of the tower of Santo Domingo el Real, which became the property of the Dominican nuns in 1513. The demigod, to whom the foundation of so many Spanish cities has been ascribed, was no doubt worshipped here.

This ancient town of warlike people is surrounded by high walls, reared by the settlers of Count Raymond in the eleventh century, though the Alcazar, the 'Casa de Segovia' (adjoining the fine old Puerta de San Juan), and the 'Tower of Hercules' just mentioned, all forming part of the enceinte, may have been in the first instance of Roman origin. The wall is strengthened by bastions and towers of various shapes —square, round, and polygonal—some with brick archings and ornamental courses of brick and plaster. The wall and towers preserve their battlements. The 'allure,' or rampart walk, is in parts so narrow as hardly to permit of safe walking. Among the most picturesque gates is that of San Andrés. It lies between two towers, one square, the other larger and polygonal, and crowning the very edge of the declivity; from one to the other runs a gallery, supported by a semicircular arch. This gate was restored by Ferdinand and Isabel, and at one time afforded ingress to the Jewry of Segovia. The masonry of the adjoining wall resembles that of the aqueduct close by, and may possibly be a fragment of the Roman fortifications.

Segovia, we are often reminded, looks like a ship in full sail towards the west; and the Alcazar is at the prow. Whether or not it occupies the site of a Saracen or Roman work, there can be no doubt that the present structure was founded by the conqueror of Toledo, Alfonso VI., at the end of the eleventh century, and was remodelled and enlarged by Juan II. in the fifteenth. Much of it is now entirely modern, the interior of the fabric having been completely restored after the fire of 1862. For all that, this citadel of Segovia remains a fine typical castle of Castile, the castle-land. The massive Torre de Juan Segundo forms the east part of the building. Its four sides are furnished with the bartizans characteristic of Spanish castles, which spring out of the wall at about half its height, and rise considerably above the battlements. Between them runs a machicolation carried on corbels. The windows in this magnificent tower are sheltered by quaint stone canopies; and the whole façade is covered with plaster, on which Gothic tracery has been stamped with a mould as at the Alhambra. The interior is vaulted, and has three floors.

Around the inner court were disposed the royal apartments, which indeed still exist, though the fire and consequent restoration have shorn them of most of their beauties. Don J. M. Quadrado, who saw them before the catastrophe, declares they were of magical splendour. A curious story is associated with the Sala del Cordon. In 1258 the learned king, Alfonso X., discoursing at the Alcazar as was his wont with a party of sages, remarked, like Lafontaine's Garo, that if the Creator had consulted him he would have turned out a better world; others have it that he declared his belief that the earth revolved round the sun, and not the sun round the earth. Whatever he said, he was rebuked for his profanity by Brother Antonio, a Franciscan. But the king hardened his heart. That very night, as he lay in bed, a thunderbolt came crashing through the ceiling, and sent him quaking and beseeching absolution to the feet of the friar. In memory of this event he decorated the walls of this apartment with the cord or girdle of St. Francis, which perhaps as a member of the lay 'Third Order' he was entitled to wear.

Passing through the handsome Sala del Trono, we reach the Sala de los Reyes, adorned before the conflagration with an ancient and valuable series of effigies of the early kings of Leon and Castile. From one of the windows Pedro, a son of Enrique II., fell out of the arms of his nurse, and was dashed to pieces on the rocks below. The woman, rather than face the king's anger, threw herself after her charge and met the same fate.

The part of rock at the western extremity of town and citadel is defended by the strong Torre de Homenage, which was held for Isabel the Catholic by Andrés de Cabrera in 1476 when the rest of the fortress had been seized by the partisans of Juana. In 1507, on the contrary, it offered a vigorous resistance to the same Cabrera, to whom, however, the garrison surrendered on May 15. The tower is surmounted and strengthened by seven turrets. The irregular disposition of these *cubos* and *torreones* (round towers and bartizans) round the four sides of a keep is a peculiarity of Spanish military architecture. Here they used to be crowned with peaked roofs of slate, probably like those that lend such a bizarre appearance to the palace at Cintra. This feature, like the plaster-work on the façade, shows distinct Moorish influence, and encourages the belief that the castle was modelled on that of the Muslim lords of Toledo.

We have seen how important was the part played in the history of the kingdom by this grand old citadel. I must not forget to mention that Le Sage places here the scene of the confinement of Gil Blas before his marriage; but as is well known, the author of the most famous of picaresque romances never set foot south of the Pyrenees.

The space to the east of the Alcazar was formerly occupied by the old cathedral, built in the twelfth century, and totally destroyed by the Comuneros in 1520. It was determined to erect the new cathedral on a more convenient site, and on the 8th June 1522 the Bishop, going in procession, laid the foundation-stone of the existing building on the west side of the Plaza Mayor. The plans were drawn by Juan Gil de Hontañon, and are very similar to those of the new cathedral at Salamanca, of which Hontañon was architect, though he is said to have used another's designs. Street thinks (and few will disagree with him) that this is the finer cathedral of the two, chiefly because its eastern end is semicircular and not square. It is one of the very latest Gothic cathedrals, and is on the whole a beautiful building in fine warm-hued stone. The plan is that of an oblong, rounded at the eastern end; or, to be more precise, it includes a nave with aisles, into which on both sides open chapels placed between flying buttresses, and a chevet with seven polygonal chapels. The choir occupies the customary position in the middle of the nave. A cupola, 220 feet high, rises over the crossing. The length of the church is given as 330 feet, the breadth as 158 feet, the nave being 44 feet across, the aisles 30 feet.

The west front is divided by buttresses into five compartments, corresponding to the nave, aisles, and rows of chapels, both in width and in elevation. The three entrances are enclosed within pointed arches. The ornamentation is restrained and pure. At the southern corner the front is flanked by a square tower 345 feet high and 35 feet in area, with six rows of windows enclosed within arcades and all blinded except those of the belfry. The angles of the platform are adorned with pinnacles, and the tower is surmounted by an octagonal clock-story. Higher than the Giralda of Seville and broader than the Tower at Toledo, this structure is a matter of legitimate pride to the Segovians.

The rest of the exterior closely resembles that of Salamanca—'the same concealment of the roofs and roof-lines everywhere,' laments Street. The outside of the chevet exhibits an excess of ornamental work; it is, in fact, a forest of pinnacles. On the south side the façade is partly hidden by the cloister and sacristies.

The interior is bright and altogether pleasing. The columns are massive and gracefully moulded, and the arches lofty. The nave and aisles are lighted by windows filled with beautifully-coloured glass. There is no triforium, but instead a balustrade in the flamboyant style in front of the clerestory of the nave.

The lantern or cupola over the crossing, and the gorgeous reredos behind the High Altar, are quite out of keeping with the general aspect of the church. The chancel is enclosed by three very fine iron screens, quite Plateresque in character, though executed in 1733. The majority of the stalls in the choir were designed for the old cathedral, half a century at least before its destruction. The organ on the Epistle side, now enclosed in an eighteenth-century case, also came from the old church, and was the gift of Enrique III. The rich marble retablo at the west end of the choir was given by Carlos III., and enshrines in a silver reliquary the ashes of the local martyrs, Fruto and his brethren.

The chapels are not specially interesting. Those in the chevet are exactly alike, and furnished like those in the aisles, for the most part, with seventeenth-century retablos. In one (Nuestra Señora del Rosario) is buried Doña Maria Quintana, who ended a dissipated life in the odour of sanctity on August 16, 1734. Her epitaph runs: 'Hic vespere et mane et meridie laudes Deo reddidit, et vitandi crimina zelo preces et lacrymas Juges effudit ; hic quam intra chorum psallere secum prohibuit, extra chorum fructuose psallere Spiritus docuit; hic tertio ab obitu die nondum rigida membra, à juncturis suis jamdiu separata quiescunt ossa.

An forsan post mortem etiam prophetabunt?' The chapel of St. Hierotio was dedicated to that saint by Bishop Escalzo under the false impression that he was the founder of the see. The Capilla de la Piedad (fifth in the left aisle) is remarkable for a fine Descent from the Cross, a retablo with colossal and expressionful figures, painted by Juan de Juni in 1571. In the same chapel is a painting by Alonso Sánchez Coello, the Apparition of Christ to St. Thomas, spoilt by injudicious re-touching.

On the south side of the cathedral is the cloister, which belonged to the old church, and was reconstructed here in beautiful flamboyant style by Juan Campero in 1524. It is entered by a fine Gothic doorway, in the Consuelo chapel (wherein is the noble tomb of Bishop de Covarrubias). On the cross-vaulting of the cloister may be seen the arms of Bishop Arias Dávila. We notice the monuments of three of the architects—Rodrigo Gil de Hontañon (died 1577), and his successors, Campo Agüero and Viadero. In the chapel of Santa Catalina at the foot of the West Tower are contained the remains of little Prince Pedro, with his painted and gilded effigy. The superb monstrance preserved in this chapel was designed in 1656 by Rafael González. At the northern aisle of the cloister may be read this inscription: 'Aquí está sepultada la devota Mari Saltos con quién Dios obré este milagro en la Fonzisla. Fizo su vida en la otra iglesia, acabó sus dias como Católica Cristiana, Año de 1237.' (Here is buried the devout Maria Saltos, with whom God performed a miracle at Foncisla. She passed her life in the other church, and finished her days as a Catholic Christian in the year 1237.) 'The other church' was of the Hebrew persuasion, to which Maria belonged. Accused of adultery, and condemned to die by the elders of her community—which was a self-governing body in Spain within certain limits—she was cast from the Peña Grajera, the Tarpeian Rock of Segovia. At the supreme moment she was heard to invoke the Virgin of the Christians, and reached the ground unharmed. She was baptized, and died, as the epitaph testifies, a devout Catholic. The incident may be ranked with the remarkable, if not miraculous, escape of the Catholic secretaries at Prague, known as the Fenstersturz.

The chapter-house, adjacent to the Western Tower, is a very splendid apartment, paved with marble, upholstered with crimson velvet, and containing some good engravings, mostly

Flemish. An elegant staircase leads to the library above.

At the back of the cathedral is the Plaza Mayor, one of the most picturesque squares in Spain. The Ayuntamiento with its Doric columns looks strangely out of place, surrounded as it is by old houses with projecting upper stories and wooden loggias of a Gothic, almost German character. The church of San Miguel may be attributed to Hontañon or one of his assistants. It replaces an earlier structure, in the porch of which the town council used to meet. In the north transept is an interesting triptych, where St. Michael is represented weighing souls. Hard by, at the corner of the Calle Ancha and Calle de los Huertos, is the old mansion of the Arias Dávila family, with a tall square turreted tower, adorned in its lower stages with diapered plaster. Near the church of San Martin are another fine tower belonging to the Marquis de Lozoya, and the house (now a book-shop) of Juan Bravo, one of the three leaders of the Comuneros.

The church of San Martin is approached by a flight of steps, and encircled on three sides by a cloister or portico, which was used in the twelfth century, at all events, as a burial-ground. The west porch is bold and original, with statuary in the jambs of the doorway, and capitals carved with birds in couples. The church was originally apsidal, but has been frequently restored. The Bravos and Rios, two prominent families of Segovia, are buried here; and the tomb of Gonzalo de Herrera and his wife in alabaster is in a chapel on the left-hand side. The church is surmounted by a modern cupola over the crossing, and by an ancient tower placed, oddly enough, over the middle of the nave.

Near the Puerta de San Martin is the Casa de los Picos, which was acquired and rebuilt in the fourteenth century by the family of Hoz. It seems once to have been known as the Jews' House, till in the sixteenth century its façade was rebuilt with the extraordinary facetted stones from which it derives its present name. While in this neighbourhood, the few poor remains of the palace of Enrique III. should be inquired for.

Where the Calle Real opens into the Plaza Mayor is situated one of the most interesting churches in Segovia. Corpus Christi Church was till the year 1410 a Jewish synagogue. In that year a rabbi obtained from the sacristan of San Facundo a consecrated Host as a security, it is said, for a loan. The street where this impious transaction took place is still known as Mal Consejo. The Jews attempted to profane the Sacred Wafer in their synagogue, but were scared by awful portents, and confessed their crime. Their place of worship was forfeited, apparently at the suggestion of St. Vincent Ferrer, and consecrated as a Catholic church. It bears a strong likeness to Santa Maria la Blanca at Toledo. The nave and aisles are separated by horseshoe arches springing from fir-cone capitals, above which runs a series of blind windows. The ceiling is of wood. The transept and dome have been added since the adaptation to the purposes of Christian worship. The sacristan will point out the crack in the wall which occurred at the moment of the attempted sacrilege.

Santa Trinidad, on the north side of the Plaza Mayor, is a Romanesque church of the San Martin type. It is adjoined like the latter by a portico, also used once as a place of sepulture. The apse is lit by three windows, below which are others now only to be seen from the interior. A lane leads from this church to San Nicolás, close to the walls. Here the two apses are each lit by a single window, and over the smaller of the two is raised a low tower with two round-arched belfry windows. The secularised church of San Facundo exhibits similar characteristics. It contains a not very valuable museum.

Segovia is a Paradise for the ecclesiologist, but so many of the churches differ only in the smallest particulars from the San Martin and San Millán type that a description of each would be tedious. An exception must be made as regards San Esteban, opposite the Episcopal Palace, famous for its Romanesque tower, the finest work of the kind in Spain. The base of the tower is as high as the nave; the remaining five stages are adorned on each side with graceful arcaded windows. The angles are splayed off, and up the middle runs a shaft. The tower is surmounted by a pinnacle, evidently a later addition, and in very bad style. The external cloister of San Esteban is the most beautiful in the town.

In the disused church of San Juan de los Caballeros are buried the founders of the two great houses of Segovia, Fernán Garcia and Dia Sanz, averred by tradition to have been the conquerors of Madrid.

The finest specimen of these early Romanesque churches is to be seen outside the south wall. San Millán is said to have been founded by the

Counts of Castile in the tenth century, but the present fabric dates from the twelfth. The church consists of a nave, aisles, and external cloisters on each side, all ending in eastern apses. There is a low, square lantern over the crossing, and a modern square tower at the east end of the north cloister. The west front is very simple and pierced with a round-arched door and four windows. The arches of the cloister spring from finely sculptured capitals on double shafts. Street calls attention to a local peculiarity in the design of the north and south doors. 'Their jambs consist of shafts set within very bold, square recesses; and the number of orders in the arch is double that of those in the jamb, they being alternately carried on the capitals of the shafts, and upon the square order of the jambs. The effect is good. . . .' The interior is well preserved, but daubed all over with whitewash and plaster. The church is barrel-vaulted, but may once have had a flat timber roof. The capitals of the massive columns are carved with very large and striking figures of men and animals. The corbels are adorned with masks and caprices, very skilfully chiselled.

Two other exceedingly interesting churches

are also outside the city wall, in the valley of the Eresma. Descending by a very steep path from the Alcazar to the junction of the two streams, and passing an arch in the baroque style, we reach Fuencisla—the bubbling rock, from which water filters. Here a cypress marks the spot where Maria del Salto alighted uninjured from the crag above. The neighbouring church, built in 1613, contains the shrine of the wonder-working Virgin of the Fuencisla. It possesses a fine reredos and iron pulpit. In the convent of the Discalced Carmelites are preserved the head and body of the famous St. John of the Cross, the spiritual guide of St. Teresa, and one of the world's greatest mystics. You may also see the pictured Christ which, it is alleged, spoke to the saint, bidding him ask a favour; John asked, as a devout Spaniard of that time might have been expected to do, for more suffering and humiliation. The cave in which he retired to pray may also be visited.

Proceeding up the valley of the Eresma, we notice the old Casa de Moneda, or Mint, built in 1586, which down to 1730 coined all the money of Spain. Above it lies the curious little church of Vera Cruz, built in 1204 by the Knights Templars, more or less on the model of the church of the Holy Sepulchre at Jerusalem. It would be difficult to convey a clearer idea of the peculiar conformation of this structure than by Street's description: 'The nave is dodecagonal, and has a small central chamber enclosed with solid walls, round which the vaulted nave forms a kind of aisle. This central chamber is of two stories in height, the lower entered by archways in the cardinal sides, and the upper by a double flight of steps leading to a door in its western side. The upper room is vaulted with a domical roof which has below it four ribs, two parallel north and south, and two parallel east and west, and it retains the original stone altar arcaded on its sides with a delicately wrought chevron enrichment and chevroned shafts. The upper chapel is lighted by seven little windows opening into the aisle around it. A slab indicates the position of the supposed sepulchre. The room below the chapel has also a dome, with ribs on its under side. On the east side of the building are the chancel and two chapels, forming parallel apses, to the south of which is a low steeple, the bottom stage of which is also converted into a chapel. The chapel in the centre of the nave is carried up and finished externally with a pointed roof, whilst the aisle is roofed with a lean-to abutting against its walls. There are pilasters at the angles outside, small windows high up in the walls, and a fine round-arched doorway on the western side.' The sepulchre is placed on the upper story, as at Jerusalem, where the hill of Calvary has been included within the church. Note the red crosses recalling the original owners, and the fast disappearing paintings on the retablo in the chancel. The portion of the True Cross formerly preserved here was removed to Zamarramala in 1663, when the old Templars' Church was abandoned so far as religious rites were concerned.

Not far off, in a desolate spot once described as a terrestrial paradise, stands the church of El Parral, the chapel of a suppressed monastery of the Hermits of St. Jerome. It was founded in 1447 by the famous Juan Pacheco, Marquis of Villena, on the ground where he had defeated three antagonists in a protracted duel. The architects were Juan Gallego and the brothers Guas of Toledo. The plan of the church is unusual. The transept is very broad from east to west, and projects but little beyond the nave. The chancel is shallow, and its lateral walls run slant-wise to the eastern angles of the transept. Most churches of the Order of St. Jerome, according to a Spanish writer, were built this way. The effect is good. The nave is practically covered by a western gallery, and has but few windows; whereas the transept and chancel are flooded with light through six tall lancet windows with statues of the Twelve Apostles in their jambs. The contrast of light and shadow is very striking and beautiful. The choir or western gallery is carried on graceful arches and is handsomely panelled. Over the north-western chapel of the transept is the organ loft. The reredos behind the High Altar, in five stages separated by columns, was painted in 1553 by Diego de Urbina. The tombs of the founder and his wife lie on either side of the chancel. Their kneeling effigies, though sadly damaged and defaced, remain among the most beautiful examples of Spanish sculpture. Equally deserving of praise is the tomb of the Marquis's natural daughter, the Countess de Medellin, in the south transept. The exterior of this church is not remarkable. The west front is pierced by a good double door, and 'adorned' with two huge square coats-of-arms; it is flanked by a square tower pierced by rounded windows in the belfry story.

Near to a cave where St. Dominic was accustomed to mortify the flesh, the Catholic Sovereigns built the church and convent of Santa Cruz, on the site of the first monastery of the order. The church has been truly described as a debased copy of El Parral. The western doorway is elaborate. Over the door, enclosed within a trefoil arch, is a Deposition from the Cross, with Ferdinand and Isabel kneeling on either side. Above, their escutcheons are displayed on either side of the crucifix. The retablo by Herrera, with which Philip II. endowed the church, was burnt in 1809, the fire irretrievably damaging the whole interior. Santa Cruz has now been converted into a charitable asylum.

Following the line of the city wall, we pass the church of San Lorenzo—a good example of the local style—once surrounded by thriving looms, and re-enter the town by the Plaza del Azoguejo, a picturesque space where the citizens love to forgather in the shadow of the mighty aqueduct.

IV

ZAMORA

ZAMORA on the Duero is one of the most picturesque towns in Spain, and one of the most celebrated in its annals. It is not well known to foreigners, probably on account of it being so difficult of approach. Few places bring back so vividly the stirring past of Castile.

The town stands above the Duero on a rocky ridge, the castle and cathedral occupying the western extremity. The river is spanned by a bridge of seventeen arches, defended near either end by a high gate-tower. If the approach is quaint and mediæval, the view from this point is even more so. Towards sundown, the spirit of the Middle Ages seems to inform the town—all is sombre, fierce, strong, and venerable. The country round seems little better than a desert. From the walls above eyes seem to be scanning the horizon for the first gleam of hostile lances. Zamora belongs to the days when towns, like men, always wore armour. To-day she is broken and war-worn and old; but if her sword is rusted and her shield broken, she may well boast it was in the service of Spain.

As we jolt over the old bridge, above the weirs of the Duero, and climb the steep street that leads into the town, we need no consultation of the records to tell us that we are here in the old Castile of the knightly days, that we shall find few memories of artists and poets, few of statesmen and great rulers, but many of hard fighters and holy priests. Zamora is constantly mentioned in the *Romancero*. We can imagine that it was a town towards which Don Quixote would have been drawn, but he only spoke of it as famous for bagpipes. Like Burgos and Valladolid and Salamanca, it was the creation of the mediæval time, and we hear first of it in the ninth century. Alfonso I., or his son Froila, took the town from the Moors. Thereafter, for many years, it continued to change hands. The Day of Zamora, famous in Spanish song and story (July 9, 901), when nearly seventy thousand Moors were slain or captured, assured the possession of the town to the Christians. In this terrific engagement Bernardo del Carpio is supposed to have won his spurs, though (if he ever existed, or the battle really took place) he must have been a hundred years old at the time! Soon after this victory the citizens clamoured for a spiritual shepherd, and a hermit named Atilanus was given them as bishop. Certain episodes of his youth began to trouble the prelate's mind, and at the end of ten years he laid aside the pastoral staff, and declared himself unworthy of his office. He went on a pilgrimage, having thrown his episcopal ring into the Duero, proclaiming that he would not return till it was restored to him as a sign that God had pardoned him. All in the least familiar with folklore will, of course, know what happened next. Like the ring of Polycrates, like the ring in the arms of Glasgow, the bishop's annulet was found in the body of a fish served up to him at supper. The relief of the good man at this unmistakable evidence of the Divine forgiveness, his return to his See, and the rejoicings of the inhabitants may be inferred and imagined. Atilanus was canonised by Urban II. in the eleventh century.

Of another tremendous victory said to have been won before the walls of Zamora in 939 over the pertinacious Moors we need not speak further, for it is more than probable that the fight never occurred here at all, but at Simancas. There can, however, be no doubt that the place fell before the irresistible Al Mansûr in 981, in spite of the brave resistance of the commandant, Domingo Sarracino. The Moors repeopled the town, which was governed by one Abu-l-Was el Tojibita. It was labour wasted so far as they were concerned, for Zamora was soon, and finally, recovered by the Spaniards. And now we come to the episode which has secured the town so prominent a place in the annals and legendary lore of the country.

Fernando I., King of Leon and Castile, in response to the importunities of his children, on his deathbed divided his dominions between them. To his eldest daughter, Urraca, he gave Zamora, to her sister, Toro. The disposition of his estates made, the dying king invoked the vengeance of Heaven on whomsoever should disturb it; and all present, except his eldest son Sancho, responded, Amen. It was not long before this prince (now King of Leon and Castile) showed his dissatisfaction with what Ford, with a touching faith in the sanctity of primogeniture, calls this unjust division. Toro was soon surrendered by Doña Elvira, and, very shortly after, the stout-hearted Urraca beheld from these walls the hosts of Castile beleaguering her little principality. With Sancho's army was the Cid. With him, the chroniclers assure us, the Infanta was in love. If so, these tender sentiments were not allowed to interfere with the vigour of the attack and defence, which were both conducted with ferocious determination. The siege had lasted seven months when a personage called Bellido Dolfos, the son, delightfully enough, of Dolfos Bellido, sought an audience of the king. He had fled from Zamora, he said, to escape the vengeance of Urraca's minister, Arias Gonzalo; and he would show the king the secret postern in the walls by which he had escaped, and by means of which the town could be taken. This audience appears to have taken place very close to the walls, for we are told that the citizens cried out to Sancho, adjuring him to have nothing to do with Dolfos, who had committed four acts of treason already. These well-meant hints, naturally enough, confirmed Sancho's confidence in the stranger. On the morning of the 7th October 1072 the two went forth to reconnoitre the walls. Dolfos took advantage of the king in an unguarded moment, and stabbed him in the back. He then promptly ran towards the postern. The Cid, seeing him run, suspected something amiss, and mounting Babieca gave chase; but alas! he had forgotten his spurs, and the assassin made good his escape. Sancho was carried back to the camp, and before he expired attributed his destruction to his father's curse. The siege was prosecuted with greater vigour than ever by his captains. Don Diego Ordoñez denounced the citizens, without exception of persons, as felon knaves. Arias Gonzalo and his four sons took it upon themselves to vindicate the honour of the town in five successive duels with the Castilian. Three of the Zamoran champions were slain by Ordoñez, but he was jerked out of his saddle by his dead adversary's wounded horse, and the combat was declared by the judges to be at an end. The venerable Arias Gonzalo thus preserved one of his sons, and Castile her champion. The accession of Alfonso VI. to his murdered brother's throne restored peace to the distracted kingdom, and left the Infanta in enjoyment of her little state.

Zamora is still encircled with massive walls, strengthened with numerous round towers. The name of Urraca's Palace is given to a house, old enough to all seeming, close to one of the gates opening near the northern end of the Paseo de Valorio; this gateway is flanked by two bastions, and above it may be seen the bust of Princess Urraca, with the inscription much defaced—

> 'Afuera, afuera Rodrigo
> El soberbio castellano!
> Acordórsete debiera
> De aquel buen tiempo pasado,' etc.

These verses from the *Romancero* are supposed to have been addressed by the Princess to the Cid, and allude, presumably, to the love-passages between them. The postern through which Dolfos escaped may be seen in the wall farther towards the west. The site of the Cid's house is also pointed out. The tiny hermitage of Santiago in the Vega marks the spot of the assassination, and a battered cross on a pillar some distance outside the town commemorates Sancho's exclamation that he would never be king till he was lord of Zamora.

The castle from which perhaps Urraca and Arias Gonzalo looked across at Sancho's camp is at the western extremity of the town. During the civil wars that disturbed the reign of Alfonso el Sabio, it was held for the king by Doña Teresa Gomez, wife of Garci Perez Chirino. Her youngest child was captured by the rebels, and to save his life she surrendered the fortress. At the time of the disputed succession following the demise of Enrique IV., the castle was held by the Portuguese in the interests of Juana 'la Beltraneja,' who held her court here for a brief season. The garrison resisted many determined assaults, and capitulated on honourable terms only after the battle of Toro, February 1476. In after years, and especially during the Peninsular War, the stronghold was adapted to the requirements of modern warfare, and has lost, in consequence, much of its mediæval character.

Hard by is the cathedral, far away from the centre of the town. When the See was restored by Alfonso VI., Gerónimo, the Cid's confessor, was appointed to it; but he was soon translated to Salamanca (or else Zamora was carved out of that See), and was succeeded by another Frenchman, Bernard, a namesake and countryman of Bernard, Archbishop of Toledo. These foreigners introduced the Romanesque style, of which Zamora must, in its primitive state, have been a noble example. The building was completed in 1174. To that period belongs the grand square tower at the west end of the north aisle—the most conspicuous landmark of the vicinity—with its three upper stories pierced on each side with one, two, and three windows respectively. The tower was designed for defence as well as ornament. Over the crossing rises a dome of beautiful construction, very Oriental in character, with turrets surmounted by smaller cupolas and pierced with rounded windows at its angles. Seen from within, this dome is of the 'half-orange' type, the ribbing of the vault giving it very much the appearance of the sections of the fruit. In the sharp fringe of ornament at the angles, Street saw the very earliest kind of suggestion of a crocket, and was of opinion that 'we have in England no monument of the middle ages which is one whit more precious.'

The cathedral has no west front, and its exterior is, it must be confessed, a veritable patchwork of different styles. The Puerta del Obispo, facing the Episcopal Palace, in the south transept probably dates from the twelfth century. The main entrance is through a four-ordered arch with three shafts in each jamb. The capitals are roughly moulded and have abaci. Over the lateral doorways (now closed up) are rudely-carved reliefs, with dragons and floral devices introduced into the decoration. The two odd-looking rosette-like ornaments above seem to be models of the interior of the dome. Above the three doors runs a gallery of five recessed arches, and over this again a blocked-up window.

The northern entrance, surmounted by a modern clock-tower, is, incongruously enough, in the classical style, with a rounded arch. The interior of this interesting little cathedral is impressive. We are at once struck with the width of the piers (seven feet across) as compared with that of the nave, which is only twenty-three feet. The arches here are in the Pointed style. The aisles are lower than the nave, and supported by broad massive buttresses. There being no western portal, that end of the church is occupied by chapels, which give a very singular effect to the building.

The High Altar and chancel are in the Gothic style, and owe their construction to the absentee bishop Diego Meléndez Valdés, who ruled the See between 1496 and 1506. His arms, five fleurs-de-lys, may be seen on the railings. The retablo, with its jasper columns and gilded capitals, is modern. The subject is the Transfiguration. In the precinct of the High Altar is buried Count Ponce de Cabrera, one of the Emperor Alfonso's most distinguished lieutenants. The Altar is in the late Gothic style, and must have been erected three centuries after the Count's death. There are good wrought-iron pulpits on each side of the chancel.

The choir was also the work of Bishop Valdés. It occupies the bays west of the crossing as usual in Spanish churches, but the bad effect of that position is here greatly relieved by the piercing of the western screen or *trascoro* with two elliptical doorways, between which is a painting representing Christ surrounded by the Blessed. The fittings of the choir are very interesting, and of the same age as the screens. The backs of the lower range of stalls are carved with low reliefs of thirty-eight personages of the Old Dispensation, from Abel to Nebuchadnezzar, Caiaphas, and the Centurion. In their hands are scrolls containing texts, very cleverly chosen, of which a list is given in Neal's *Ecclesiologist*, and reprinted in Street's *Gothic Architecture in Spain*. The execution is rude, but expressive and painstaking. The upper stalls are adorned with full-length reliefs of saints, confessors, and martyrs of the New Dispensation, which are more delicately designed and finished. Above runs a canopy, sculptured with animal forms. The enormous metal lectern and the Bishop's Throne, with its tapering spire, are fine examples of Gothic work.

The chapels are not of special interest. That on the middle of the western wall is dedicated to San Ildefonso, but is more generally known as the Capilla del Cardenal, after its founder, Don Juan de Mella, who died in 1467. This prelate's brother, Alonso de Mella, was the founder of a sect which seems to have resembled the Anabaptists of Westphalia; he was expelled from Castile, and took refuge at Granada, where he was put to death by the Moors. The retablo, by Gallegos, is in six divisions, the subjects being: San Ildefonso receiving at Toledo the chasuble from the hands of the Blessed Virgin, the Discovery of the Relics of St. Leocadia, the Veneration of the Relics, and (above) the Crucifixion, the Baptism of Christ, and the death of John the Baptist. This chapel contains the tombs of the Romero family. In the adjoining sacristy are some interesting battle-scenes from Old Testament history.

The chapel of San Juan Evangelista was built with funds bequeathed by Canon Juan de Grado (1507), whose fine alabaster tomb is surmounted by his recumbent effigy, accompanied by a priest and an angel. Above the canopy is an exquisitely chiselled composition representing the Crucifixion, with expressive statues of the Apostles Peter and Paul; within is a curious but admirable genealogy of the Blessed Virgin, at the base of which is the recumbent figure of an old man, wearing a crown, and representing possibly one of the early patriarchs. The Capilla de San Miguel is of less interest. It contains the sixteenth-century tombs of the canons de Balbas. Of the side-chapels, the most notable is that of San Bernardo, rebuilt in the sixteenth century.

In the sacristy is preserved a remarkable silver monstrance, six feet high, attributed by Ford to Enrique de Arfe. The stand is of later construction, and dates from 1598. On the upper part the local saint, Atilanus, may be seen, seated with the Saviour and the Virgin.

The original cloisters were burnt in 1591, and rebuilt in the present Doric style in 1621 by Juan de Mora.

Under the town walls, close to the cathedral, is the little Romanesque church of San Isidoro, noticeable for its extremely narrow windows, some mere slits in the masonry.

We pass down the long lane-like street which leads into the town, and which in the sixteenth century was the scene of desperate conflicts between the Mazariegos and Monsalves, the Montagues and Capulets of Zamora. The first church passed is that of San Pedro, rebuilt by

Bishop Meléndez Valdés, and containing the revered ashes of St. Ildefonso, which were discovered here under miraculous circumstances in the year 1260. The relics of St. Atilanus are also preserved here. Nothing remains of the primitive Romanesque structure, except a little apse on the Epistle side, and a closed-up doorway in the left wall. The originally-distinct nave and aisles were thrown into one at the restoration, and form overhead one immense span. The sacristy contains some interesting objects—sacred vessels and altarpieces of the sixteenth and seventeenth centuries.

Presently we reach the second most interesting church in the town, La Magdalena, a small Romanesque work, said on rather doubtful authority to have been built by the Templars about 1312. The southern doorway is very large in comparison with the edifice. It is deeply recessed between massive buttresses, and formed by a rounded arch with shafts curiously moulded and twisted. Street speaks of this as a very grand example of the latest and most ornate Romanesque work. The carving on the arches is very rich. Above is a large rose window, resembling those in our own Temple church. The interior of the church is architecturally but not æsthetically more interesting than the exterior. The nave has a flat wooden ceiling. The apse is groined, and the chancel has a waggon-vault. The stone pulpit against the north wall is a notable piece of work, but attention at once becomes riveted on the large canopied tombs at the entrance to the chancel. Both are square-topped, with round arches and capitals very purely and vigorously carved. They are generally asserted to date from the thirteenth century, but an inscription over one describes it as the sepulchre of one Acuña and his wife, who died in the fifteenth century. 'The effect of this monument,' says Street, 'filling in as it does the angle at the end of the nave, is extremely good; its rather large detail and general proportions giving it the effect of being an integral part of the fabric rather than, as monuments usually are, a subsequent addition.'

Another canopied tomb against the north wall undoubtedly dates from the earlier period. The capitals of the three twisted shafts are carved with the forms of wyverns fighting. The tomb is closed by a stone on which is a large cross. The occupant—believed by some to have been a Templar—is shown on his deathbed, while above him his soul—represented by a winged head—is borne away by angels. This interesting work may be attributed to a native sculptor acquainted with the art of France and Italy.

Santa Maria la Horta (or de la Huerta), near the river, was modelled, like the Magdalena, on the cathedral. Apart from its architectural peculiarities—the western tower, narrow windows, waggon-vaulting of the chancel, etc.—it is of interest on account of the retablos and paintings in its chapels. Here, as at the very similar church of San Leonardo, the roofing of the nave is not flat but arched, which goes to support Don J. M. Quadrado's belief (opposed to Street's) that the flat roof of La Magdalena is an innovation.

The church of San Juan in the Plaza Mayor is in the Flamboyant style. Its most curious feature is a Christ Crucified near the west door, surrounded by human skulls built up in the form of a cross. Hard by is the early Gothic church of San Vicente, with a noble square tower in three stages, and a fine west front.

In a town like Zamora only two kinds of buildings were esteemed—churches and fortresses. Time has spared few important civil monuments. The only ancient house of note is that styled the Casa de los Momos, of which I give an illustration. The heavy stones forming the arch suggest a Castilian architect. The building dates from the sixteenth century, as the enormous coat-of-arms over the entrance might have prepared us to expect. The Ayuntamiento, or Town Hall, in itself devoid of interest, contains some good paintings by Ramon Pedro y Pedret, illustrating the history of the city. It will be seen that Zamora, like almost every other Spanish town, is entitled 'most noble and loyal' (*muy noble y leal*). It is a sombre, fascinating place, where the past is more easily recoverable by the fancy than in many cities more richly endowed with ancient monuments.

V

AVILA

LIKE Stratford-on-Avon, like Assisi, this sombre city in the mountains of Castile is the shrine of a single pre-eminent personality. To the Spaniard Avila is essentially the city of the great saint—of Santa Teresa, the greatest, perhaps, of Spain's many great women. And the fame of the saint and, therefore, of the city, has spread far beyond the limits of the country in which she was born, and indeed outside of the church to which her every faculty was devoted. To those (and they are in the large majority) who approach Avila as pilgrims, it may seem idle to tell anything of its story unconnected with her. At Assisi you wish to hear only of Francis, and who cares aught for the Stratford of an earlier day than Shakespeare's?

But Teresa was the product of Avila, and to the making of her character all the experience and emotion of her ancestors had contributed. Those who would rightly understand her must know something of the breed from which she sprang.

The city is one of the forty-three said to have been founded by Hercules. It is mentioned, indeed, by Ptolemy, but we know nothing of its history previous to the reconquest of this part of Castile by Alfonso VI. Avila, like Salamanca and Segovia, arose from the ashes of the Moorish empire, and was repeopled and probably rebuilt by the Count Raymond of Burgundy. To him we owe those venerable walls, stern yet beautiful in their ruddy granite, that girdle the city round. But these served, at a very early date, to keep out other than the infidels. The annalists tell us that the knights of Avila, returning one day from a foray, found that the Moors had ravaged the neighbouring country and carried off a multitude of prisoners and much booty. Without hesitation the enraged gentlemen gave chase, and though the enemy were in vastly superior numbers, they overtook and routed them at Barbacedo, recovering most of the spoil and a good deal of additional treasure. But, on their return to Avila, the ungrateful commons closed the gates against them, and refused admittance to the deliverers of their own wives and children unless they were given a large share of the booty. The indignant knights refused to surrender the guerdon of their swords, and entrenched themselves in the suburbs. Peace was restored only on the intervention of Count Raymond, who expelled the churlish townsmen and intrusted the government of the city to the knights. During the whole of the twelfth century the bitterest animosity continued to prevail between the descendants of these antagonists.

Heroines are common in Spanish history. When the town was unexpectedly besieged by the Almoravides in the absence of nearly the whole male population, the women garrisoned the walls wearing the men's helmets, and compelled the enemy to withdraw. The leader of these Amazons was Jimena Blásquez, wife of the governor, Fernán Lopez. Her female descendants were privileged, in remembrance of this event, to speak and to vote at the council board in the same way as men.

Jimena's kinsman, Nalvillos, was as unfortunate in love as he was fortunate in war. One day he saw Ayesha Galiana, the beautiful daughter of the late Moorish king of Toledo. Desperately enamoured, he forgot his own betrothal to Galinda Arias, and that the fair infidel had been promised to her countryman, Jenina Yahya. With the favour of the king he overcame all these obstacles, and made Ayesha his wife. But she could forget neither her old faith nor her old love. Nalvillos' deeds of prowess failed to win her heart; and one day he returned to Avila from a victorious expedition to find that the bird had flown. She had returned to her first love, Yahya, who had raised the standard of revolt at Talavera. The furious Castilian stormed the town, slew the Moor, and penetrated to his faithless wife's bower, only to find her expiring from a self-inflicted wound. Nalvillos lived many years after, and fought and won many battles. He rose to great distinction in the service of his sovereign, but we never hear of his marrying again.

It was in this town, that styles itself *del rey, de los leales, de los caballeros*, that the boy king Alfonso VIII. was placed by the Regent, Don Manrique de Lara, to protect him from his uncle, Fernando of Leon. But the class rancour of Avila was not unknown to Fernando, who stirred up the people of the suburbs against the *serranos*, or aristocratic townsfolk, promising them a share in his new town of Ciudad Rodrigo. The knights were victorious, and do not seem to have conducted themselves with great generosity towards the vanquished.

The inveterate hostility of the commons did not tend, as it might be expected to have done, to unite the threatened ranks of the patricians. These prosecuted bitter feuds among themselves, different families striving desperately for the mastery. One faction, on being expelled from the town, took refuge in a neighbouring castle, where they were surprised and cut to pieces by the Moors.

The place was regarded, notwithstanding, as the safest asylum for the boy-kings who so often appear in the pages of Castilian history. During his minority, Alfonso XI. remained in the custody of the bishop till the pretenders to the regency had adjusted their claims to his lordship's satisfaction. In the Civil War of 1367 Avila was on the right side—that of Enrique II.—and suffered severely in consequence at the hands of the Black Prince's marauding hordes. Here at the Puerta del Alcazar took place, at the instance of Carrillo, Archbishop of Toledo, the mock deposition and degradation of Enrique IV., represented by an effigy, and the proclamation of his eleven-year-old son as king. Yet in 1474 the fickle city displayed every sign of grief and remorse on the unfortunate monarch's death.

In the disputed succession that ensued Avila sided with Queen Isabel. Possibly as an expression of royal gratitude, the convent of Santo Tomás was chosen for the first seat of the Tribunal of the Inquisition; and in 1491 three Jews, professing the faith of their fathers to the last, were roasted to death in the Mercado Grande.

Avila was the seat of the Supreme Junta of the Comunidad from July to September 1520. The rebellious temper of her citizens found expression in Philip II.'s reign in some anonymous placards, posted in the streets, reflecting on the king's policy. The royal vengeance was indiscriminate and drastic. The Vicar of Santo Tomás was stripped of his sacerdotal functions, Don Enrique Davila was imprisoned for life in the castle of Turegano, and Don Diego Bracamonte perished on the scaffold. This king's successor inflicted the *coup de grâce* on the luckless town by expelling its large and industrious Morisco population. Avila never recovered her prosperity. She remains an example of the wholly destructive policy of the Spanish Hapsburgs. Not only was the country ruined by the expulsion of the Jews and Moriscos, but these exiles were not able to transplant their industry to some other clime. With their expulsion so much productive and industrial power was absolutely lost to the world. The wealth acquired by the Inquisition at the expense of its victims, or rather what was left of it, ultimately found its way into the State coffers on the establishment of the new order of things a century ago.

Avila 'of the Knights' was, before all else, a fortress. When the walls were built, churches and suburbs were left outside the enclosure, that the military advantages of the height on which the old town stands might not be lost. These walls of dark-red granite girdle Avila to-day, unbroken, formidable, intact. They rise so high that they shut out from view all that they enclose, except the towers of the cathedral. Near San Vicente the masonry is fourteen feet thick, and forty-two feet in height. Flanking defence is provided by eighty-six elliptical towers—thirty on the north, twelve on the west, twenty-five on the south, twenty-one on the east. These rise above the crenellated parapet at places by eighteen feet. The ten gateways are formed by two towers being brought together and connected with arches. The most impressive gates are the Puertas del Mercado and de San Vicente, the former admitting to the scanty remains of the old Alcazar, the latter facing the church of San Vicente. In both cases the flanking towers are connected at the level of their platforms by a high, arched and crenellated gallery. The actual gateway is defended by a portcullis, and the usual apertures for thrusting out lances, beams, etc. One of the gates, now walled up, was known as the Puerta de la Mala Ventura, in memory of a baseless tradition that it was the scene of the massacre by Alfonso el Batallador of certain Avilese nobles who had been given him as hostages for the little King Alfonso VII. of Castile. Nearly all the gates open on to squares or places of arms. A leisurely walk round these grand old walls is one of the most agreeable experiences of a journey in Spain, and carries the mind back to the days when knighthood was in flower. From their strength it is easy to see how the town could have been held by a limited number of Caballeros against the commoners of the suburb outside. There seems no reason to doubt that the walls were, as tradition avers, built by Raymond of Burgundy in the last decade of the eleventh century. Eight hundred men were employed upon them daily during nine years, under the direction of a Roman, Cassandro, and a Frenchman, Florin de Ponthieu.

Built into the city wall at its eastern end is the noble cathedral of San Salvador, founded according to some by Fernán Gonzalez, Count of Castile, and begun a second time in 1091 by Alvár Garcia of Estella in Navarra. It is, perhaps, the finest example extant of the fortress-church of the Middle Ages. The oldest part is the apse, which makes a pronounced bastion or projection in the city wall. The external walls probably date from Alvár Garcia's time, but the rest of the church must be from one to two centuries later.

The church consists of a nave, aisles, projecting transepts and a chevet, which has semicircular chapels built into the town wall and double aisle. The chevet is, architecturally, perhaps the most interesting part of the structure. Nothing at all is to be seen without of the chapels, over which is carried the ordinary rampart walk or allure; behind this rises a second battlemented wall, from which we look down on to the aisle roof of the chevet and clerestory of the central apse. This end of the cathedral appears from the exterior simply as an unusually massive round tower projecting from the wall. The west front is flanked by two towers, only one of which—the northern—is completed. This is a notable and fortresslike structure, recalling similar work in England. The strongly-defined buttresses finish in pinnacles, and are outlined at the angles with a ball enrichment, which is also to be seen on the pointed arches over the belfry windows. The windows themselves are round-arched, as are also those now filled up in a lower stage of the tower. The entrance is comparatively modern. On either side is the figure of a wild man with shield and mace—strange guardians of a church! On the spandrils of the arch are the figures of Saints Peter and Paul. The middle stage of this front is occupied by a curious retablo-like composition. In the various compartments are the figures of Christ and different saints, sheltered by ugly canopies; and surmounting this work is an extravagant and tasteless acroterium, displaying the arms of the Chapter. Behind and above this is the older and infinitely more graceful west window within an elliptical arch, and with delicate though elaborate traceries.

Very much finer is the north porch, admitting not to the transept but to the nave. The elliptical arch has on each side six jambs, each of which is adorned with the figure of an apostle resting on the capital of a pilaster and sheltered beneath a canopy. The five orders of the arch are sculptured with reliefs of angels and prophets, alternating with wreaths. In the centre of the tympanum is the seated figure of Christ; and around Him, arranged in four horizontal divisions, are compositions representing the Betrayal and Last Supper, the Coronation of the Virgin, and the Angelic Choir. Street recognises in this doorway the work of the architect of the portals of the cathedrals of Leon and Burgos. Before it are two lions couchant on pedestals, chained to the walls. The porch dates from the fourteenth century. Above it is a canopy begun in 1566, and intended to form a kind of triumphal arch. Crowning all is seen the figure of the Redeemer.

The north transept is pierced by a fine wheel-window of sixteen divisions. The windows of the clerestory are very large, and placed between great double flying buttresses. Since 1772 the upper and lower traceries have been blocked up, for a reason not apparent to the modern observer. The windows of the transept escaped this treatment, and are filled with good stained glass.

The nave is 130 feet long and 28 feet broad.

The arches are supported by piers of four pilasters, the capitals of which show Romanesque influence. The aisles are only about half the height of the nave, and are 24 feet wide. Their pitched roof formerly admitted light into the nave through the triforium, now blocked up.

The outer walls of the chevet, as we have seen, are the most ancient part of the fabric, but the seven chapels formed within the thickness of the wall are of later date. The extraordinary beauty of this part of the church is due to the division of the ambulatory into two by a series of tall, slender columns carrying some excellent groining. The outer or recessed aisle is narrower than the inner, an inequality corrected very skilfully at the opening into the south transept by an imperceptible deviation in the line of columns. Very little light penetrates through the narrow slits in the chapel walls into this sombre, beautiful arcade.

Behind the reredos of the High Altar sleeps the learned bishop, Don Alonso Fernández de Madrigal, surnamed el Tostado and el Abulense, who died in 1455. The prelate, who was one of the most prolific writers that ever lived, is shown in alabaster writing at a desk. The framework of the tomb is adorned with reliefs of the Adoration of the Magi and Shepherds, of the Divine and Cardinal Virtues, and of the Eternal Father. This noble work has been variously ascribed to Berruguete and to Domenico Fancelli, whose more famous performance we shall see in the church of Santo Tomás.

In the chapel of Santa Ana is buried Don Sancho Davila, Bishop of Plasencia, who died in 1625. Most of the tombs in the chapels of the chevet belong, however, to the thirteenth century, though the dates on most of them are merely conjectural, and were inscribed in the sixteenth century by a prebendary of the cathedral.

The High Altar is backed by an elaborate retablo of the age of the Catholic Kings. It is divided into three stages, and was painted by Pedro Berruguete (father of the more famous Alonso), Santos Cruz, and Juan de Borgoña (father of Felipe). To the two first-named may be attributed the ten panels of the lowest stage, representing Saints Peter and Paul, the Four Evangelists, and Four Doctors of the Church, and the Transfiguration, Annunciation, Nativity, Adoration of the Magi, and Presentation in the Temple, in the second stage. To Borgoña we may ascribe the Agony in the Garden, the Scourging, Crucifixion, Descent into Hell, and

Resurrection, in the third stage. To the right and left of the church are two beautiful Rennaissance retablos in alabaster, illustrating the lives of Saints Secundus and Catharine, and two tasteful gilt iron pulpits. The light reaches the High Altar through two rows of thirteen windows, the lower 'round-arched, of two horseshoe-headed lights divided by a shafted monial,' and the upper 'round-headed, broadish windows, with jamb-shafts and richly-chevroned arches.' The fine stained glass is the work of Albert of Holland (1520-1525).

The choir was placed in the easternmost bay of the nave in 1531. The *trascoro* or back of the choir is adorned with reliefs of the Adoration of the Magi, the Massacre of the Innocents, and the Presentation; smaller panels represent other scenes from the history of Christ and the Blessed Virgin. The frieze with its fourteen figures of prophets is the finest part of the work. The choir stalls were begun in 1527 by Juan Rodrigo, and completed by Cornelius of Holland in 1536. The carving is of varying merit. The upper panels appear to portray the martyrdoms of different saints, episodes in whose lives are shown on the panels below. The ornamentation of the columns and friezes is profuse and delicately done.

In the south transept is the fine tomb of Don Sancho Davila, Bishop of Sigüenza, who died in 1534, and near him that of a namesake, whose effigy is clad in armour. This knight died before the walls of Alhama in a combat so furious that his scattered limbs had afterwards to be collected and pieced together by his friends. A curious tomb is to be seen near by: the figures of a knight in armour and an ecclesiastic repose on black coffins, the sides of which are sculptured with escutcheons upheld by woolly-haired savages; a monkey is seen pulling the negroes' hair. In the chapel of San Miguel, at the north-west end of the nave, is an interesting tomb of the thirteenth century, representing a funeral, whereat the anguish of the mourners contrasts strikingly with the stoical indifference of the clergy.

The gorgeous chapel of San Segundo at the south-east of the apse, outside the town wall, was founded in 1595 by Bishop Manrique, on the model, it is said, of the Escorial. Magnificence, rather than good taste, characterises this chapel and its furniture. Frescoes by Francisco Llamas illustrate the life of the saint, whose ashes are contained in a Churrigueresque tabernacle. On the opposite side of the apse, but within the wall, is another excrescence, the Velada chapel, completed in the eighteenth century.

The sacristy is an ornate Renaissance structure, richly gilded and painted. The alabaster retablo over the altar of St. Barnabas is the work of a genius whose name unfortunately has not been handed down. The chamber also contains some curious fifteenth-century paintings relating to the life of St. Peter. Here may be seen the superb monstrance of Juan de Arfe, dated 1574, and therefore among his earliest works.

The cloister on the south side of the cathedral was built in the early sixteenth century on the site of an earlier one. There was an attempt made at the same time to restore, more or less at haphazard, all the tombs and epitaphs left from earlier times. At the angles are chapels, one of which, the Piedad, contains some good stained glass and iron-work. East of the cloister is the spacious apartment called the Cardinal's Chapel, after Cardinal Davila y Mujica, whose tomb it contains. Here met the Junta of the Comuneros. The fine stained glass in the windows shows the skill of Juan de Santillana and Juan de Valdevieso, two famous glass-workers of Burgos.

In some respects more interesting than the cathedral, and probably more ancient, taken as a whole, is the Romanesque church of San Vicente, outside the walls, near the Segovia gate. It marks the site of the martyrdom of Vicente and his sisters, Sabina and Cristeta, who had taken refuge here to escape the persecution of Dacian, at the beginning of the fourth century. Their religion having been discovered, they were again apprehended, and put to death by their skulls being battered against the rocks. Their bodies were left unburied, but a great serpent came out of a hole near by and protected them from insult. A Jew approached the spot, led by spiteful curiosity, and was seized by the monster, which wound its coils about him. The terrified Hebrew invoked the name of Christ and was released. He was baptized, and secretly gave the martyrs honourable burial, subsequently raising a church over the scene of their martyrdom. So runs the tradition. These dissenters from the state religion of the Roman Empire are remembered and revered to this day, and magnificent fanes are rightly raised over their graves. Their ashes are preserved in reliquaries more costly than royal thrones, and kings kneel before their shrines. But no monuments are erected, no reverence paid to the equally high-minded and courageous dissenters from the state religion of the Spanish monarchy, who perished in the flames kindled by the Inquisition. The very city which delighted to honour Vicente and his sisters, and recorded its detestation of the lawful authority that put them to death, was the seat of the dreadful tribunal of Torquemada and the scene of cruelties worse than any perpetrated by the Romans.

The basilica raised by the converted Jew was swept away by the Moors, and the relics of the martyrs seem to have been transported elsewhere. They were recovered, at least in part, at the time of the resettlement of the city, and the present church was built by St. Ferdinand in 1252 to contain them; though parts of the fabric certainly seem, despite the absence of documentary evidence, to date from a century earlier. The church is built on sloping ground, the difficulties of the site being admirably overcome. The plan is cruciform, the nave and aisles terminating in apses. The crossing is surmounted by a square lantern, and the western front flanked by steeples. An open cloister runs along the outside of the south aisle.

The western front is very beautiful. The southern tower or steeple wants a third or upper story, which was added to the north tower only in the fifteenth century. The second stories are arcaded, and splayed at their angles. On the third gable-like story of the north steeple are hung the bells, one of which bears the date 1158. These towers open only into the western-most bay of the nave, which forms the porch of the church, opening on the outside with a high-pointed arch, and into the interior through a superb double doorway. Street speaks of this porch as follows: 'The whole effect is fine, and the light and shade admirable and well contrasted; but the charm of the whole work seemed to me to lie very much in the contrast between the noble simplicity and solid massiveness of the architecture generally, and the marvellous beauty and delicacy of the enrichments of the western doorway, which is certainly one of the very finest transitional works I have ever seen.' The shaft dividing the doors is sculptured with a figure of Christ seated on a pedestal. Statues of the twelve Apostles occupy the jambs. Over each door a round arch springs from luxuriantly carved capitals, flanked by the heads of bulls and lions. The tympana are occupied with representations of Dives and Lazarus, and the Release of a Blessed Spirit.

The round arch which encloses the whole portal exhibits a marvellous profusion of delicate and rich ornamentation. A Spanish writer truly observes that the foliage looks as if the faintest breeze would stir it; the beasts seem ready to spring, and the birds as if, with the least effort, they might disentangle themselves and fly from the branches. Over the arch is a parapet and string-course, and a round-arched window opening into the nave.

The church is usually entered by the south door opening into the aisle beside the transept. The seven orders of the archivolt are almost devoid of ornament, but the capitals are carved with curious figures of wild beasts fighting. The monogram of Christ on the keystone of the innermost arch is rare in Castilian churches, and the rude sculptured figures on the capitals are very primitive and unsymmetrical. On one of the jambs the Virgin and the Angel Gabriel are sculptured; on another a curious mitred personage representing, it is believed, one of the ancestors of the Messiah.

This porch is older by two centuries than the cloister running along the south side of the church. It is in twelve semicircular arches, with a buttress between every three. Made of purple granite, it contrasts strikingly with the sandstone of the main edifice.

The north front is very plain and severe. The massive buttresses excited the enthusiasm of Street. The north door is of corresponding simplicity. Beside it, as at the side of the south door, are a couple of tombs, which seem to prove that the space round the church was at one time used as a burial-ground.

The eastern end is the most interesting part of the building. The central apse is larger and loftier than the adjoining apses. All three are divided perpendicularly by slender engaged shafts, terminating in capitals under the eaves; and horizontally by carved or moulded string-courses. The central apse has three round-headed windows; the lateral apses, two each. The capitals and corbels are everywhere very finely carved. There are few better examples of Romanesque work in the Peninsula. The square lantern is pierced on each side with a three-light window of Gothic design. At its angles it is surmounted by stone crosses.

The interior is impressive and thoroughly Romanesque. The piers are square, and rest on round bases. The capitals are carved with oak leaves. The arches are semicircular, and the vaulting pointed. Between two string-courses runs a triforium of round-arched openings, the windows of the clerestory being likewise rounded and of one light. The windows of the aisles have been closed up. The church is undergoing extensive repairs. The piers of the lantern seem to be of later date than the foundation of the church, and seem to indicate that the original lantern had at one time fallen in. The interior is octagonal, and pierced with four lancet stained-glass windows. On the chancel side is a fine fourteenth-century painting of the Crucifixion, with the Virgin and Disciples.

The interior of the central apse is occupied by the High Altar, with an ugly baroque retablo which unfortunately conceals the graceful windows.

The shrine of San Vicente and his brethren is placed on the south side of the crossing. In the ages of faith this was an object of extraordinary sanctity. Men were sworn on the tomb, and it was universally believed that the arms of those who bore false witness thereon withered away. The practice was forbidden by law under Ferdinand and Isabel. Notwithstanding, grave doubts existed as to the actual whereabouts of the martyrs' bodies. To set the matter at rest, the Bishop Martin de Vilches, in the reign of Enrique III., decided on a thorough examination of the tomb. Having celebrated Mass, he caused the sarcophagus to be opened. Dense vapour immediately issued forth, and the bishop thrust in his hand, to withdraw it a second later, convulsed with a violent pain, and covered with blood. He proceeded no further with the investigation, and ordered the tomb to be closed, satisfied that it contained the holy relics. The imprint of his blood-stained hand was left on a tablet placed inside the arches on which the sarcophagus rests. This appears to date from the thirteenth century, and is carved with interesting reliefs. The baldachino covering it is carried on four bold columns, and was added by Bishop de Vilches, whose arms it bears. The figure at the apex appears to represent San Vicente.

In the south transept is a tablet with an inscription declaring that there lie the remains of the Jew who gave the martyrs decent burial. Close by is the shrine, executed by Francisco de Mora, of San Pedro del Barco, a saint of absolutely unknown antecedents, and mentioned as far back as 1302.

The crypt has been modernised. On it may

be seen the rock on which the tutelary saints suffered martyrdom, and a miraculous image, called Nuestra Señora de la Sotteraña, which is obviously far from possessing the antiquity its devotees claim for it.

Characteristics very similar to San Vicente are exhibited by the church of San Pedro in the picturesque Mercado Grande. Dating from the latter part of the twelfth century, we find here also the apsidal east end, the square lantern, and the entrances at the west end and beside the transepts. The western porch is very fine, and above it is a very beautiful wheel-window. The north doorway is more richly sculptured, and is later than the rest of the fabric. There are a few points of difference between this church and that previously described. There is no triforium, and the clerestory windows are of a single light, and much larger than those of the nave. As at San Vicente, the apsidal chapels have been spoilt by injudicious painting. In the transept are the tombs of the rival families of Blasco Jimeno and Esteban Domingo, distinguished by shields of six and thirteen bezants respectively. The church is in every respect a noble edifice, but loses interest after you have visited the almost identical basilica of San Vicente. Nor will your attention be long engaged by the modern monument to the illustrious natives of Avila in the centre of the market-place, crowned by the statue of Santa Teresa. Here took place in 1491 the *auto da fé* of the Jew, Benito Garcia, found guilty of murdering a Christian child, and stealing a consecrated Host for the purpose of sacrilegious rites. It should be added that no particular child could be put forward by the prosecution as having been murdered, and the suppositious victim went down to posterity simply as the Niño de la Guardia— la Guardia being the village where the crime was supposed to have taken place. The body was conveniently assumed to have been taken up to heaven. Its disappearance did not benefit the luckless Hebrews, two of whom, before the execution of Garcia, were torn to pieces by red-hot pincers.

The town proper having always been regarded as an acropolis, the greater number of churches are situated outside the walls. Several of these, like those already described, are of considerable interest. The doughty Nalvillos is said to lie beneath the flags of the church of Santiago. San Andrés is an interesting Romanesque structure, spoilt, however, by the addition of an incongruous sacristy. To the north-west of the town, near the river (Adaja), is the curious little sanctuary of San Segundo, with a wooden roof, and rather suggestive of Norman architecture. It marks the spot whereon fell an unfortunate Saracen, who was pushed over the turret above by the sainted Secundus. Some of the ashes of that muscular Christian are preserved here, beneath the fine alabaster statue which represents him kneeling with an open book before him. The sanctuary is believed to occupy the site of the earliest Christian church of Avila. The actual edifice is not nearly so old as the ruined and abandoned church of San Isidoro, now fast crumbling away.

One of the most important monuments of the city is the church of the Dominican monastery of Santo Tomás (now used as a missionary college). It was founded in 1478 by Doña Maria Davila, wife of a Viceroy of Sicily, and completed in 1493. Torquemada, the Grand Inquisitor, interested the Catholic sovereigns in the work, and the cost was met by the confiscated property of Jews and heretics. The cloisters and conventual buildings are devoid of interest. The west front is in a poor late Gothic style, and distinguished by richness rather than beauty. The two massive flanking buttresses are outlined with a ball ornament, and end in eaves, corbel tables, and paltry pinnacles. Beneath the gable is a huge escutcheon, and beneath this again a round window. The doorway is within a deep porch; the archivolt is pointed and elaborately fluted and carved; on either side of the doorway are statues of saints of the Dominican order beneath canopies. The interior is more interesting. The chancel is almost square, the transept short; and, curious to relate, not only is the choir placed in a gallery in the western nave, but the altar is correspondingly elevated at the eastern end. Street thought the effect of this arrangement very fine, an opinion which all are not likely to share. The reredos is tastefully carved and painted. The choir stalls are good, as usual in Spain, particularly the royal chairs, which have splendid canopies, and bear the device of the yoke and sheaf of arrows.

Interest here, however, centres mainly in the superb Renaissance monument to the Infante Juan, eldest son of Ferdinand and Isabel, who died at Salamanca in 1497, aged nineteen. Ferdinand, to soften the blow, caused his wife to be informed that he and not the prince had perished; and such, in Isabel's temperament, was the excess of conjugal over maternal affection, that her relief when the real state of things was revealed to her enabled her to bear the loss of her son with comparative composure. The tomb was the work of Domenico Alessandro the Florentine, specimens of whose skill we have seen in the cathedral. At the corners of the sarcophagus are eagles; the sides are covered with reliefs of the Virgin and the Baptist, and of the Cardinal and Theological Virtues. On the edge of the upper slab are carved escutcheons, angels, trophies, and garlands. The recumbent effigy of the prince, crowned, and with sword and mantle, is marvellously well done. The sculptor has expressed adolescence in stone. This rightly ranks among the finest works of art in Spain. Hardly inferior is the tomb of Juan Davila and his wife, Joana Velazquez de la Torre, the prince's attendants, also by the Florentine. Don Juan is shown clad in somewhat fantastic armour; a page kneeling at his feet holds his helmet. Sphynxes are placed at the corners of the sarcophagus, the sides of which bear medallions representing St. James destroying infidels, and St. John the Divine in a cauldron of boiling oil.

In the sacristy is a tomb more impressive than

either of these, but in a very different sense. A plain slab covers the body of Tomás de Torquemada, Grand Inquisitor of Spain. He lies here in the temple reared on the fortunes of the men and women he had plundered and burned. There is no inscription to tell us who rests here; but Torquemada is as little likely to be forgotten as Attila or Nero. Few things in Avila create a deeper, sadder impression than the tomb of this strange, sinister priest.

His was one phase of the religious temperament, not perhaps more difficult of comprehension to us modern northerners than Teresa's. We execrate the one and revere the other, and understand neither. Still, we know enough to see that the Inquisitor and the Nun stand respectively for what is worst and best in the Spanish character. And, happily, the woman's fame has far outshone the man's.

We may assume that no one who visits Avila is ignorant of the leading events in her career, or needs to be told what manner of woman she was. What we have to do is to follow her footsteps through her native city. The house in which she was born on March 28, 1515, has been converted into an ugly church (Nuestra Seráfica

Madre Santa Teresa de Jesus). The exterior is in the baroque style. The room in which she first saw the light is now a chapel in the worst taste, and contains her rosary, sandals, and even one of her fingers. It was from this house that she stole away with her brother Lorenzo, determined to seek martyrdom at the hands of the Moors. Here she indulged in those 'worldly conversations' and that light reading which to her carefully polished conscience in after years appeared fraught with such dire peril. Here her vocation was born; and to this house she returned from the cloister in after years to watch by the deathbed of her father, Alonso de Cepeda.

It was in the Carmelite convent of the Incarnation, north of the city, that Teresa took the veil on All Souls' Day 1533. Nothing remains of the structure as it was in her day. More interesting is the convent of 'Las Madres,' which occupies the site of the first foundation of the reformed order. The poor chapel of St. Joseph gave way in 1608 to the present handsome church designed by Francisco de Mora, who spared the tomb and chapel of Teresa's brother, Lorenzo. Other fine monuments are those of Bishop Alvaro de Mendoza, and of Francisco Velazquez and his wife. In the garden of the convent is shown an apple-tree planted by the saint. Her body does not rest here, but at Alba de Tormes, where she expired on October 15, 1582.

You may also visit, for her sake, the church of San Juan in the Mercado Chico, where she was baptized on April 7, 1515.

Attached to the Dominican convent is the sumptuous chapel of Mosén Rubio de Bracamonte, which was founded by Doña Maria de Herrera in 1516. The architecture represents the transition from late Gothic to Renaissance. The interior is richly adorned with marbles, the semicircular windows with stained glass. The tomb of the patron (Mosén Rubio, lord of Fuente del Sol) and his wife is in keeping with the splendour of the edifice, which is further enriched by two ancient paintings of Saints Jerome and Anthony of Padua. The reredos dates from the early seventeenth century.

The dark granite of which the houses of Avila are built gives them a spurious air of antiquity. Very few date from before the age of Charles v. Near the cathedral is the mansion of the Marquis de Velada, whose ancestor, Gomez Velada, entertained the Emperor here in 1534. Opposite is an interesting doorway, with the figure of an armed knight, surrounded by escutcheons and enclosed within a trefoil arch. A magnificent doorway, likewise sculptured with armed figures and overhung by a kind of bartizan, leads into the fine courtyard of the palace of the Condes de Polentinos. An interesting house is that of the Davilas of Villafranca. The escutcheon with thirteen bezants between two chained slaves, supported by mounted heralds, was won by the family in an expedition to Ronda. At the side is a picturesque window with a grating, above which is the inscription *Petrus Davila et Maria Cordubensis uxor MDXLI.*, and beneath, in Spanish, 'Where one door shuts another opens.' The houses of the Bracamontes and of the Counts of Superunda deserve notice.

VI

ZARAGOZA

WHILE certain cities may lay claim to having been at one time or another the capital of the united kingdom of Leon and Castile, and while, in fact, two often held the rank at the same time, Zaragoza, from its reconquest by the Christians to the unification of the Spanish monarchy, was the undisputed capital of the kingdom of Aragon. We must not expect on that account to find that it was any more amenable to the royal authority, or any less turbulent than the cities of the sister state. On the contrary, nowhere in the Peninsula was liberty more highly prized or more strenuously vindicated, than in the chief city of Aragon. And it holds what out of Spain, at any rate, will be considered the honourable distinction of having offered the most determined resistance to the establishment of the Inquisition. Many cities in the dominions of His Catholic Majesty are entitled to style themselves 'most heroic.' None assuredly deserve the description better than this, the Numantia of modern Spain.

An Iberian town seems to have existed here from the remotest times, and to have been known as Salduba. On its annexation by the Romans, it was rechristened Caesaraugusta, and under that name is referred to by Pompeius Mela as the most famous of the inland cities of Tarraconensis. Christianity took root here at an early date. Bishops of Caesaraugusta are mentioned by St. Cyprian, and the local martyrology includes the names of Saints Valerus, Vincent, and Engracia. When, in the year 542, Zaragoza was besieged by the Franks under Childebert, the exposition of the relics of these martyrs is said to have sufficed to propitiate the enemy and to preserve the town from destruction.

In the year 713 the city opened its gates to Muza, the Moorish invader, without, as Don Francisco Codera believes, striking a blow. The Crescent reigned over Zaragoza for four centuries. During that time there were many changes of rulers. The blood of martyrs again watered the soil under the cruel Wali, Othman Aben Nasr, though generally throughout the period of Muslim domination the Christians enjoyed the same freedom as their co-religionists, under the same yoke, in other parts of Spain. Their principal church having been converted into a mosque, San Pablo was, during this period, their place of worship.

In the year 778 occurred the famous expedition of Charlemagne, around which an almost impenetrable veil of poetry and legend was woven through the Middle Ages. Hoseya al Arabi having been superseded in the government of the city by order of the Khalifa, Abd-ur-Rahman, appealed for assistance to the great Emperor of the West, who, for motives which remain obscure, entered Spain with a considerable force. On reaching Zaragoza, he found that Al Arabi had already regained possession of the city; and either on that account, or because his late ally refused to open the gates, he retraced his steps towards the north. In the pass of Roncesvalles his rearguard was attacked and cut up by the mountaineers—a reverse which has been immortalised as the occasion of the death of the Paladin Roland, and commemorated in the legendary lore of nearly every European tongue.

At the latter end of the ninth century Zaragoza (or Sarakusta, as it was called by the Moors), shook off the yoke of the Khalifas, and under the sway of the renowned Hafsûn became for a short time an independent state. More lasting was the monarchy set up at the close of the eleventh century, on the break-up of the Spanish Khalifate, by the vigorous Almundhir Ben Hud, whose power extended from Lerida to Guadalajara, from the mountains of Biscay to the Mediterranean. His son and successor, Suleyman, made the mistake of dividing his dominions among his four sons, Sarakusta being assigned to the eldest, Ahmed Almuktader. But, united or disunited, the Moors of north-eastern Spain were incapable of offering an effective resistance to the ever-growing power of the Christian kingdom of Aragon. In the spring of 1118, Alfonso el Batallador appeared before the walls of Zaragoza with a formidable host. The city held out till the garrison witnessed the total defeat of an army sent to their relief by the Almoravides. All hope being then gone, the gates were opened on December 18, 1118, and Zaragoza became the capital of the kingdom of Aragon.

As such, it was endowed with a very liberal charter—the *fuero*, of which we read so often in Aragonese history. The defence of these liberties was intrusted to twenty magistrates, who were invested with authority to deal in the most summary and drastic fashion with evildoers, whatever might be their station. Nor did they hesitate, in after years, to raze the castles of any barons who threatened the peace of the city. Domestic affairs were regulated by twelve jurates, representing the twelve parishes. Pedro II. amplified these privileges, and decreed that the municipality should not be responsible for its acts even to the sovereign.

The history of Zaragoza during the twelfth, thirteenth, and fourteenth centuries is full of instances of civil strife, of faction fights, and of struggles with the royal authority. The citizens refused to recognise Alfonso III. as king till he had been crowned within their walls. They paid dearly for their arrogance under Pedro IV., who hanged thirty of their number at the Toledo gate, and burnt the articles of the Union—a pact extorted from one of his predecessors—in a public assembly.

Under Fernando I. the city's privileges were further curtailed. But as licence and disorder showed no signs of abating, a kind of vigilance committee was formed in 1454, headed by Jimeno Gordo. This worthy put down all disturbances with iron hand, and waged war on the neighbouring barons. His career was cut short in 1474 by Ferdinand the Catholic, who caused him to be publicly executed. All the disorderly elements of the city rejoiced at his death.

The introduction of the Inquisition met with much opposition in several Spanish towns, but nowhere more than at Zaragoza. Deputations were sent from the states of Aragon to wait on the king at Valladolid, to urge upon him the withdrawal of the obnoxious tribunal, without avail. Such contemptuous indifference to the laws and wishes of the people of Aragon roused the Zaragozans to a dangerous pitch of exasperation. About midnight, September 14, 1485, a party of six men entered the cathedral, and found the Inquisitor, Pedro de Arbues of Epila, in prayer before the altar. They at once transfixed him with their swords and knives, but only a few of the blows struck home, thanks to the shirt of mail which the victim, like most of the Inquisitors, wore beneath his cassock. The deed, of course, only riveted the chains of the Holy Office more firmly upon the Aragonese.

Most of the assassins were captured, and perished in the flames. De Arbues was canonised in 1664. There can be no question that the Inquisition was established contrary to the laws of the country, and that the man met his death through presuming to discharge unlawful functions. He died for having broken the law, his executioners for having vindicated it.

The persistent encroachments of the Crown upon their constitutional rights during the next century met with strenuous resistance from the people of Aragon. The long-impending storm burst in 1590. Antonio Pérez, having incurred the anger of Philip II., fled to Zaragoza, and invoked the protection of the states. According to the *fueros*, he was then confined in the prison of the Manifestacion pending his trial. But the Holy Office impudently removed him from the custody of the law, and threw him into their prison of the Aljaferia. A popular tumult followed. Pérez was released and taken back to his first prison. The Viceroy, the Marqués de Almenara, died of chagrin, it is said, at the insults he had received from the crowd. Four months later a fresh riot broke out, and enabled Pérez to make good his escape to France.

Philip now sent an army of 14,000 men into Aragon to re-establish his authority on the ruins of the constitution. The Justiciary, Juan de Lanuza, summoned the people to defend their country. But the Castilians dispersed this hastily collected force at the first encounter, and entered Zaragoza unopposed on December 12. Juan de Lanuza and many other persons of note were judicially murdered; the leaders of the aristocracy were imprisoned, and the city sacked from end to end.

Never again did Zaragoza raise its head in defiance of the King of Spain. The *fueros* continued nominally in force till 1707, when they were formally abrogated by Philip V. in revenge perhaps for the defeat sustained before the walls at the hands of Stanhope and Stahremberg. But the spirit of the people was far from being crushed. They might bow before their own king, but they would not bend the knee to a foreigner. Zaragoza's defence in 1808 is one of the most glorious episodes in the history of the nation. When the revolution broke out at Madrid on May 2, the citizens expelled the Governor, Guillelmi, and elected as leader Don Jose Palafox, a young noble of great personal courage and charm. He was assisted by a priest named Santiago Sas, his secretary Boggiero, who is said to have penned all his proclamations, and by three peasant leaders, 'Tio' Jorge, 'Tio' Marin, and Mariano Cerezo. All their equipment for war consisted at the outset of 220 men, a few muskets, and sixteen guns; yet when Lefebvre Desnouettes arrived before the place on June 15, he met with so stubborn a resistance that he was compelled to proceed cautiously. He reduced the city indeed to a heap of ruins, but he had not taken it when Dupont's surrender at Bailen obliged him, on August 15, to raise the siege.

The French reappeared in December 1808, to the number of 18,000 men, under the command of Marshals Lannes, Moncey, Mortier, and Junot. The city was attacked on two sides at once, but more especially from the Jesuit convent on the left bank of the Ebro, which the Spaniards had neglected to secure. What followed may be read in the pages of Napier. The besiegers breached the wall near the convent of Santa Engracia, and the combat was continued day after day in the streets of the town. Every house was held as a fortress, every few yards of street was defended by a barricade. In answer to the summons to surrender rang Palafox's defiant 'War to the knife and to the last ditch!' The women in many cases fought beside the men. When Maria Agustin saw her sweetheart fall at his post, she took the linstock from his hand and fired the gun herself. The fame of this 'Maid of Saragossa' has penetrated every land. For twenty-one days the fighting continued in the streets. Finally, on February 21, 1809, the defenders capitulated on honourable terms. The town was a smoking heap of ruins and of dead. Zaragoza had shown an astonished world that the spirit of Saguntum and Numantia yet lived in Spaniards. And, we doubt not, it still lives.

The city soon arose from the ashes. It rapidly recovered its prosperity, which took a fresh impetus on the opening of the four railways, east, west, north, and south. Here you see both the Old and the New Spain—the one with its heroic, glorious memories, the other with its promise of things as great and happier.

THE CITY

Zaragoza stands on the right bank of the Ebro in an oasis in the desert of Aragon. Nothing could be more attractive than the immediate environs, or more desolate than the country a few miles farther out. Such a situation was familiar to the Berber conquerors, who made themselves at home here and left their mark on the architecture of the city long after the last 'Tagarin' Moor had been expelled. Not, of course, that Zaragoza is to be compared as regards Musulman architecture with Seville, Cordova, Granada, and Toledo; but the Moor has left behind him unmistakable evidences of his presence, and an interesting monument called the Aljaferia, which endures, though oft and oft restored, to this day.

The name seems to be derived from Jaffir, a not uncommon name among the Moors, and borne perhaps by one of the Beni Hud dynasty, for whom the building served as a palace. At the conquest in 1118 it was allotted by Alfonso the Battler to the Benedictine order. In the fourteenth century it again became the residence of royalty, and doubtless was entirely transformed and repaired. It was the scene of great splendour at the coronation of King Martin, and of several of his successors. To-day it presents a sad and dilapidated appearance. The imposing staircase, decorated with fine stucco work, is the creation of the Catholic sovereigns, who seem to have had some idea of reconstituting the past glories of the palace in true Moorish style. The ceilings of some of the chambers are in the artesonado style —the work of fifteenth-century artificers. The most beautiful is to be seen in the Salon de la Alcoba, where was born in 1271 the sainted Princess Isabel, afterwards Queen of Portugal,

K

and persistently confounded by English writers with St. Elizabeth of Hungary. Everywhere among the decorations appear the devices and mottoes of Ferdinand and Isabel.

Genuine Moorish work is to be seen in a little octagonal chamber opening off the patio. Of the eight arches, two are in horseshoe shape, and the others formed by irregular and capricious curves. The columns are almost hidden in the walls. The ceiling is modern, and unfortunately cuts off the view of the elegant *ajimeces* and arabesques of the upper stage. The ornamentation recalls that of the Alhambra. This chamber—said by some, on no particular authority, to have been a mosque—was the seat of the Inquisition down to 1706. The guide points out a cell called La Torreta, in which—according to Verdi's opera *Il Trovatore* — Manrico was confined. The opera is founded on a legend of Zaragoza, and the libretto was written by Garcia Gutierrez, a native of the city.

Some may enjoy the beautiful view of the Pyrenees obtained from the Aljaferia more than the building itself.

Probably only a few fragments of this old palace are older than the Cathedral of La Seo.

This is the name commonly given in Aragon to the cathedral church, and comes, of course, from the Latin *sedes*, like our own word 'See.' Zaragoza became the metropolitan city of Aragon in 1318, and the archiepiscopal dignity was reserved as far as possible to the illegitimate sons of the kings. The city has now two cathedrals, which are used for alternating periods of six months. The Seo is the older of these, and occupies the site of the Moorish mosque—some say, even of an earlier Christian temple dating from Roman times. The church was, at all events, entirely rebuilt between 1188 and 1432, several Moorish names being mentioned among the architects. It can hardly be said to have been completed till the year 1550. Here were crowned the Kings of Aragon, and here, as we have related, was slain the Inquisitor, Pedro de Arbues.

The west front was completed as late as 1685 by Julian Garza and Juan Bautista Contini. It is in the classical style of that period, and is in two stages separated by a broad entablature. The lower stage is adorned with massive Corinthian columns, and pierced with three doorways; the upper story is decorated with three statues of Christ and the Apostles Peter and Paul, by Giral, placed in niches; above is a pediment finished with an ugly finial. This front is flanked by an octagonal tower of four stages, each smaller than the lower one, and is therefore not inaptly compared by Ford to a telescope. This structure is in the same style and reveals the same want of taste as the adjoining façade. The third stage contains the belfry. The whole is surmounted by a weather-vane and steeple, perched on a Moorish-looking dome. The statues of the Apostles on the belfry are by Acali. There is no other façade worthy of notice; but the Puerta de la Pavostria is in the better and earlier classic style of the sixteenth century. It derives its name from a functionary known as the Pavorde, who here distributed alms.

Street, who did not consider this cathedral in general interesting, has much to say about a portion of brickwork at the north-east angle, inlaid with small tiles in diapers, red, blue, green, white, and buff on white. The eminent architect sees in this an interesting specimen of Moorish work, and praises the grave quiet of the whole decoration (*Gothic Architecture in Spain*, xvii. 372).

The church is of unusual breadth, there being two aisles and a row of chapels on each side of the nave. 'The nave and aisles,' says the authority we have just quoted, 'are all roofed at the same level, the vaulting springing from the capitals of the main columns, and the whole of the light is admitted by windows in the end walls, and high up in the outer walls of the aisles. In this respect Spanish churches of late date almost always exhibit an attention to the requirements of the climate, which is scarcely ever seen in the thirteenth and fourteenth centuries; and this church owes almost all its good effect to this circumstance, for it is in light and shade only, and neither in general detail nor in design that it is a success.'

The vaultings are adorned with gilded pendants and bosses, very much in the Moorish style. The light red marble pavement, with rays diverging from the yellow marble bases of the columns, appears to have been intended to suggest a reflection of the roof with its ogive vaultings above. The decoration is tasteful and not elaborate. The capitals are sculptured with *putti* upholding escutcheons with animals and foliage.

Over the chancel is the lantern, octagonal in plan, which replaced an earlier one in the first quarter of the sixteenth century. The work was undertaken by Enrique de Egas, only at the express command of the king. The lower part is adorned with statues in niches, and with the canting arms (the half-moon) of the family of Archbishop de Luna.

The reredos of the High Altar is of alabaster and in the Gothic style. It was executed at the order of (and not by, as we have seen erroneously stated) Archbishop Dalmacio de Mur (1430-1456). The seven compartments are filled with compositions representing the martyrdom of St. Lawrence, the burial of St. Vincent, and episodes in the history of St. Valerus; with statues of the two latter saints, angels, and New Testament scenes. In all, the expressions and the draperies are exquisitely rendered. Don J. M. Quadrado is of opinion that this superb work was executed by Pedro Johán of Cataluña, Ans, Gombao, Gaspar, and Gil Morlán successively.

Before the High Altar the coronation took place, and the king, robed like a deacon, prostrated himself before the primate. On the gospel side is the wooden coffin which contains the ashes of Maria, daughter of *Jaime lo Conqueridor*, who died in 1267. At her side is the noble marble tomb of Archbishop Don Juan de Aragon, brother of Ferdinand the Catholic, with statues of the Mater Dolorosa, attended by Saints Jerome, Martin, and Francis. Here are also the tombs of Archishop Don Alonso, natural son of Ferdinand the Catholic, and of his natural son, also Archbishop, Don Fernando. The first-named did not take orders till after the birth of his son and successor, and only celebrated one mass, deeming himself unworthy of the sacerdotal functions. Beneath a tablet is deposited the heart of the Infante Baltasar Carlos, eldest son of Philip IV., carried off by smallpox at the age of seventeen. His portrait is familiar to students of Velazquez.

The choir occupies two of the five bays west of the crossing. It is in the Gothic style, and closed by a modern railing. In the centre is the tomb of Archbishop de Mede, from whose time the choir dates. The stalls are of Flemish oak. The fine lectern dates from 1413. The *trascoro*, or back of the choir, is a gorgeous plateresque affair in marble and stucco, the work of Tudelilla of Tarazona, who flourished about 1538. His are the statues of the martyrs Vincent and Laurence, the four reliefs illustrating their martyrdom, and that of San Valero, and the groups of cherubim. The tabernacle is in a not untasteful baroque style, and has side columns of black marble and a good crucifix. This figure of Christ is said to have addressed Canon Funes, afterwards Bishop of Albarracin, who is shown on his knees regarding it. The sides of the choir are adorned with statues of saints, including that of Pedro de Arbues, on the very spot where he was slain.

Few of the chapels are of interest, and all but one have been disfigured with baroque portals. In the chapel of San Bernardo is the fine tomb and effigy by Morlánes of Archbishop Don Fernando de Aragon, above being a retablo representing the Betrayal and the Crucifixion. Close by lies Doña Ana de Gurrea, mother of the prelate (died 1527). The chapel of San Gabriel, founded by Gabriel de Zaporta, is notable for its fine bronze *reja* and plateresque adornments. In the chapel of San Dominguito del Val are preserved 'the remains of the third child crucified by the Jews in hatred of Christ towards the year 1250'; and the chapel of San Pedro de Arbues contains that worthy's body, his kneeling effigy by José Ramirez, and paintings by Jimenez of Tarazona. In the chapel of Nuestra Señora de la Blanca are collected the tombs of sundry archbishops. The chapel of San Miguel owes its origin to a ghastly legend. Passing through the pine grove of Villaroya, the Archbishop Don

Lope de Luna heard a voice calling him. He turned and saw that it proceeded from a severed head which came leaping towards him. The decapitated man had called on the Archangel at the moment the axe descended, and life was miraculously preserved in his head till he had made his confession, and was absolved by the primate. De Luna's tomb is a triumph of Gothic art. He is shown with mitre and crozier, reclining on a sarcophagus which is sculptured with twenty-eight figures of friars in various attitudes. In niches in the wall surrounding the tomb are beautifully carved figures of ecclesiastics and grandees, full of vigour and expression. The name of the sculptor of this fine work is unhappily unknown.

In the sacristy is to be seen the Gothic cross of gold and jewel-work, on which the kings of Aragon swore to observe the *fueros*. Some of the vestments are very fine. A casulla is said to have come from old St. Paul's, London, at the time of the Reformation. There is a magnificent *custodia*, dating from 1537, and a fine silver reliquary, sent from Avignon in 1405 by Benedict XIII. (the anti-pope, De Luna). In the Sala Capitular are pictures attributed to Ribera and Zurbarán. The fine tiled pavement of this room is modern.

The church of Santiago is mentioned as far back as 1121, and retains a few Romanesque features. Here the saint is said to have lived on his visit to Spain; and in the porch the magistrates of the city used to assemble and to administer justice.

The most important church in Zaragoza after the Seo is, in Street's estimation, that of San Pablo, built in 1259. The octagonal steeple is faced with tiles in much the same way as the part of the cathedral wall above described, and is certainly a later addition to the structure. The nave is of four bays and terminates in a five-sided apse. The aisle is continued all round the church, and communicates with the nave by pointed arches in an extraordinarily thick wall. In the left aisle are five early and highly interesting Gothic retablos. The elaborate reredos of the High Altar, with its reliefs of the Passion and of the Acts of St. Paul, is hardly worthy of the master—Damian Forment—to whom it has been hastily attributed. Ford suggests that it is the work of one of his pupils.

The church of Santa Engracia, which figured prominently in the great siege, commemorates the massacre of a number of Christians of both sexes by the soldiery of Dacian. The bodies of the saints, Engracia and Lupercius, having been discovered here in 1389, the church already built on the spot was enlarged, and finally rebuilt with great splendour by Ferdinand the Catholic. A terrific explosion on August 13, 1808, completely wrecked the fabric, leaving little more than the plateresque portal, believed to have been designed by Morlánes. The entrance is through a round arch recessed within another, and surrounded by a retablo-like arrangement of niches containing groups. The outer arch is flanked by four statues of doctors of the Church in niches, and surmounted by statues of Ferdinand and Isabel.

The existing church, clumsily restored by the Hermits of St. Jerome, contains some interesting tombs of the martyrs. They appear to date from the fifth century. One is decorated with reliefs in the rudest Byzantine style, the subjects being Adam and Eve and the Serpent, and the sixteen martyrs, whose relics are enclosed. The pillar is shown at which Santa Engracia was flogged by order of Dacian, and a well which is believed to contain the bones of innumerable martyrs.

It is curious and painful how constantly the memorials of religious fanaticism confront one in this beautiful country. Here we are shown the spot where a Christian suffered for his faith;

there where a Jew perished; there where a Moor died for conscience' sake. Persecution naturally engenders a vindictive and intolerant temper in its victims, and these, become the masters, are hardened, not softened, by affliction. Religion, too, in Spain was almost always identified with race. The Moor, the Jew, and the Lutheran were not only infidels or heretics, but aliens—the political and racial enemies of the Spaniard. In fact, religious intolerance in the Peninsula cannot be said to have assumed such unnatural forms as in France and Germany, where men of the same blood and language cut each other's throats, and vied with each other in doing the most harm to their native lands.

To the dawn of the sixteenth century also belonged the famous leaning tower at Zaragoza, the Torre Nueva, now demolished; while the Lonja or Exchange commemorates the reign of Juana la Loca, or as the inscription states, of her and her son, Don Carlos, 'conregnantes' (1551). This is one of the many buildings scattered over Spain and Europe generally which were intended to accommodate brokers and business men, who resolutely refuse to swarm in the appointed spots —witness our own Royal Exchange, the Lonjas of Seville and Granada, etc. The exterior belongs to no recognised style. The round-headed door is flanked by two windows of similar shape; above runs a sort of imitation gallery, then two more rows of round-headed windows, finished off with a fine eaves-cornice. The soffits of the arches are elaborately carved. At each corner of the edifice is a little tower, roofed with white and green tiles. The interior is divided into a nave and aisles by twenty-four columns, of which seventeen are embedded in the walls. From their Ionic capitals spring seventeen arches, which at the points of intersection are studded with gilt bosses. The Lion of Zaragoza may be distinguished among the decorations, and over the door and on the walls the arms of Spain. O'Shea says that the 'gigantones'—gigantic figures representing the four quarters of the globe, carried about in processions—are kept here.

A great many of the fine old mansions (*solares*) of the aristocracy and merchants of Zaragoza disappeared in the siege, or to permit of modern improvements. Those which remain date mostly from the sixteenth century. The finest, on the whole, is the Casa de la Infanta, so-called as having been the residence of La Vallabriga, a lady banished from Madrid for marrying the

Infante Don Luis. The house was built by a rich merchant named Gabriel Zaporta in the middle of the sixteenth century. A square entrance admits to a court, round which runs a gallery, upheld by columns on fluted pedestals, and formed of caryatide figures interlocked. On these rest the capitals, elaborately carved with masks, and on these again is borne the gallery, the arches and parapet of which are enriched with medallions, masks, grotesques, and foliage. The decoration is a fine specimen of the plateresque style. The staircase, in the same style, is worthy of note.

The fine old Casa de Comercio, described in several guide-books of recent date, no longer exists. The noble mansion of the Counts of Sastago housed Philip III. in 1599; and the Audiencia occupies the site of the ancestral home of the De Luna family, to which belonged the anti-pope Benedict XIII. and the wicked Count in Verdi's opera.

We have left almost to the last that ambitious but meretricious memorial of the decadence, the new cathedral, or Iglesia del Pilar. The Apostle James (Santiago), according to tradition, visited the city forty years after the birth of Christ. He was favoured by a vision of the Blessed Virgin, poised on a pillar of jasper, and attended by angels. He built a modest chapel on the spot, which soon became a great resort of pilgrims. This was replaced in the thirteenth century by a large church, which was demolished to make room for the present building, erected in 1686 by Don Francisco Herrera. The design, bad enough in itself, was made worse by Ventura Rodriguez seventy years later. The exterior hardly merits description, though the domes or cupolas with their brilliant green, yellow, and white tiling are not without a certain bizarre beauty.

Spanish writers are as severe as others in their condemnation of this spacious edifice: 'The baroque style' (says Don J. M. Quadrado), 'as timid and clumsy in the general proportion of the work as it was audacious and presumptuous in detail, gave space not repose to the Pilar—size without grandeur. The eye measures vainly this square of 1500 feet, and observes the nave and aisles equal in dimensions; it rests on the twelve square piers—enormous masses which might serve for the bases of towers, recoils from the bare vault, from the thick cornice, from the ridiculous foliage of the capitals, the arches, etc. This disagreeable impression is intensified by the strange and confused disposition of the temple, which, divided into two by the Shrine and the High Altar, presents two centres of attraction, and obstructs the nave with objects masking each other.'

The only objects of particular interest in this vast edifice are those just named, which stand back to back. The Shrine or Capilla Santa constitutes a chapel within a chapel, the exterior being rectangular, the interior elliptical. Overhead is an oval dome borne on four Corinthian columns, with capitals richly gilded, and over this again another cupola or lantern painted by a namesake (not a relative) of Velazquez. There are four smaller domes painted by Goya and Bayeu. The profusion of rich marbles, the elaboration of the architecture, the brilliancy of the frescoes, and the multitude of statues give this chapel a sumptuous and not inartistic appearance. Around are hung banners taken from the infidels. The Sacred Pillar is almost entirely concealed, but there is a hole in the casing through which the devout may kiss it. On each side of the chapel imposing staircases lead to the crypt, in which lie several archbishops and canons, and the heart of Don Juan José of Austria, brother of Carlos II.

The High Altar of the cathedral is of alabaster and in the Gothic style, the work of one Damian Forment, an early sixteenth-century artist. The lower reliefs, separated by slender pilasters, represent the Espousals of the Virgin, the Annunciation, the Visitation, the Nativity, the Adoration of the Magi, the Crucifixion, and the Resurrection. Above, in canopied niches, are the Assumption, the Nativity, and the Presentation. The canopies are richly adorned with the figures of saints. At the sides are two large statues of St. James and St. Braulio—objects of special devotion—and at the apex of the altar-screen are two angels supporting Our Lady of the Pillar. The whole is undoubtedly the finest work of art in the cathedral.

The choir stalls merit attention. They were designed by the Navarrese Estebán de Obray, and carved by the Florentine Giovanni Moreto and Nicolás de Jobato between 1542 and 1548. The infinite number and variety of the designs, the delicacy and intricacy of the work, suggest that it was accomplished in two or more generations rather than in six years. Equally admirable is the bronze *reja* by Juan Tomás Celina (1574) on a marble base, sculptured by the Majorcan artist, Guillermo Salvá.

The sacristy contains an immense variety of

offerings to the shrine by pilgrims from all parts of the world. These had been accumulating for centuries, and the Chapter were able some years ago to raise a sum of £20,000 by disposing of only a portion of them. Without profanity we might perhaps say that the Virgen del Pilar is to Zaragoza what Diana was to the Ephesians. Hundreds make a living by selling pictures and models of the shrine, and a surprising number of silversmiths do a roaring trade in images and medals. Yet it is not quite wise or safe for the traveller to scoff at a devotion which largely inspired the heroic defence of 1808, and supplied the place of arms, strategy, and able leadership.

Close by, the yellow Ebro is spanned by the seven arches of the Puente de Piedra. Its origin is of unknown antiquity. It was here in 1435, when one of the arches collapsed—presaging the destruction by the Genoese of the Aragonese fleet which sailed that day; and the inscription mentioning Alfonso V., and the date 1437, can only refer to its reconstruction. And across this bridge we pass into the stern, desert country of Aragon, and so on to the distant, gleaming Pyrenees.

PLATE I

GENERAL VIEW OF VALLADOLID

PLATE 2

GENERAL VIEW OF VALLADOLID

PLATE 3

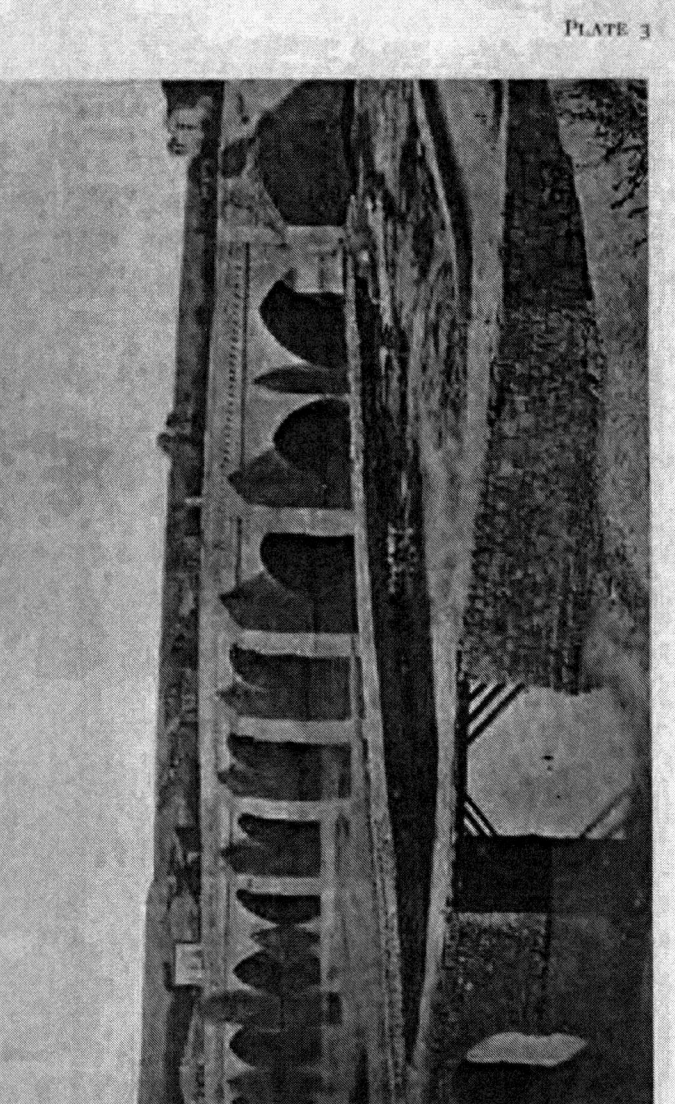

THE BRIDGE OF PIEDRA
VALLADOLID

PLATE 4

LA ACERA DE SAN FRANCISCO

PLATE 5

THE TOWN HALL
VALLADOLID

PLATE 6

THE OLD PARISH CHURCH
VALLADOLID

PLATE 7

HOUSE IN WHICH CHRISTOPHER COLUMBUS DIED, 1506
VALLADOLID

PLATE 8

HOUSE WHERE KING PHILIP II. WAS BORN, 1527

PLATE 9

THE ROYAL PALACE OF PHILIP III.
VALLADOLID

PLATE 10

CHURCH OF SAN JUAN DE LETRAN

PLATE II

COLLEGE OF THE ESCOCESES
VALLADOLID

PLATE 12

COLLEGE OF THE INGLESES
VALLADOLID

PLATE 13

INTERIOR VIEW OF THE LIBRARY
VALLADOLID

PLATE 14

INTERIOR OF THE MUSEUM
VALLADOLID

PLATE 15

FAÇADE OF THE MUSEUM
VALLADOLID

PLATE 16

PLATE 17

MUSEUM. DETAIL OF THE CHOIR STALLS OF SAN BENITO

PLATE 18

MUSEUM. SEVERAL FRAGMENTS OF CHOIR STALLS
BY BERRUGUETE
VALLADOLID

PLATE 19

MUSEUM. HEAD OF ST. PAUL. WOOD CARVING.

PLATE 20

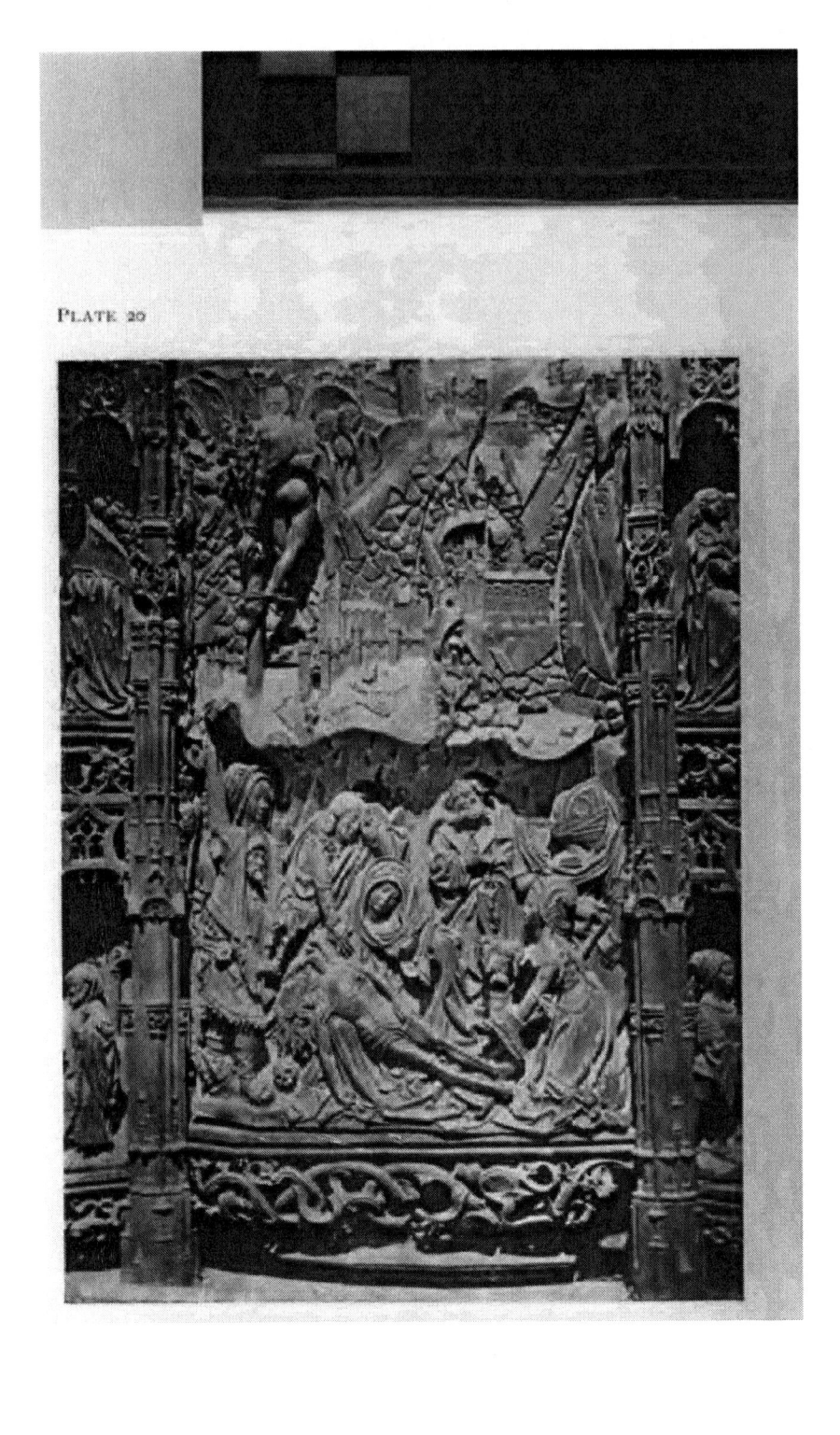

PLATE 21

MUSEUM. FRAGMENTS OF CHOIR STALLS. BY BERRUGUETE
VALLADOLID

PLATE 22

MUSEUM. FRAGMENTS OF CHOIR STALLS. BY BERRUGUETE
VALLADOLID

PLATE 23

MUSEUM. ALTAR-PIECE CARVED IN WOOD. END OF
FIFTEENTH CENTURY
VALLADOLID

PLATE 24

MUSEUM. THE ASSUMPTION OF THE VIRGIN. BY RUBENS
VALLADOLID

PLATE 25

MUSEUM. ST. ANTHONY OF PADUA AND THE
CHILD JESUS. BY RUBENS
VALLADOLID

PLATE 26

MUSEUM. THE ANNUNCIATION, BY JOSÉ MARTINEZ
VALLADOLID

PLATE 27

MUSEUM. THE HOLY FAMILY. BY RAPHAEL
VALLADOLID

PLATE 28

MUSEUM, ST. FRANCIS AND A LAY BROTHER
BY RUBENS
VALLADOLID

PLATE 29

ST. JOACHIM AND THE VIRGIN AS A CHILD
BY MURILLO
VALLADOLID

PLATE 30

PROVINCIAL MUSEUM. ST. BRUNO
VALLADOLID

PLATE 31

a.

CENTRE OF THE FAÇADE OF ST. GREGORIO
VALLADOLID

PLATE 32

DETAIL OF THE FAÇADE OF ST. GREGORIO (LEFT SIDE)
VALLADOLID

PLATE 33

DETAIL OF THE FAÇADE OF ST. GREGORIO (RIGHT SIDE)
VALLADOLID

PLATE 34

LEFT ANGLE IN THE COURT OF ST. GREGORIO

PLATE 35

GALLERY IN THE COURT OF ST. GREGORIO
VALLADOLID

PLATE 36

PLATE 37

PLATE 38

PLATE 39

LOWER PART OF THE FAÇADE OF ST. PABLO

PLATE 40

DETAIL OF THE PORTAL OF ST. PABLO
VALLADOLID

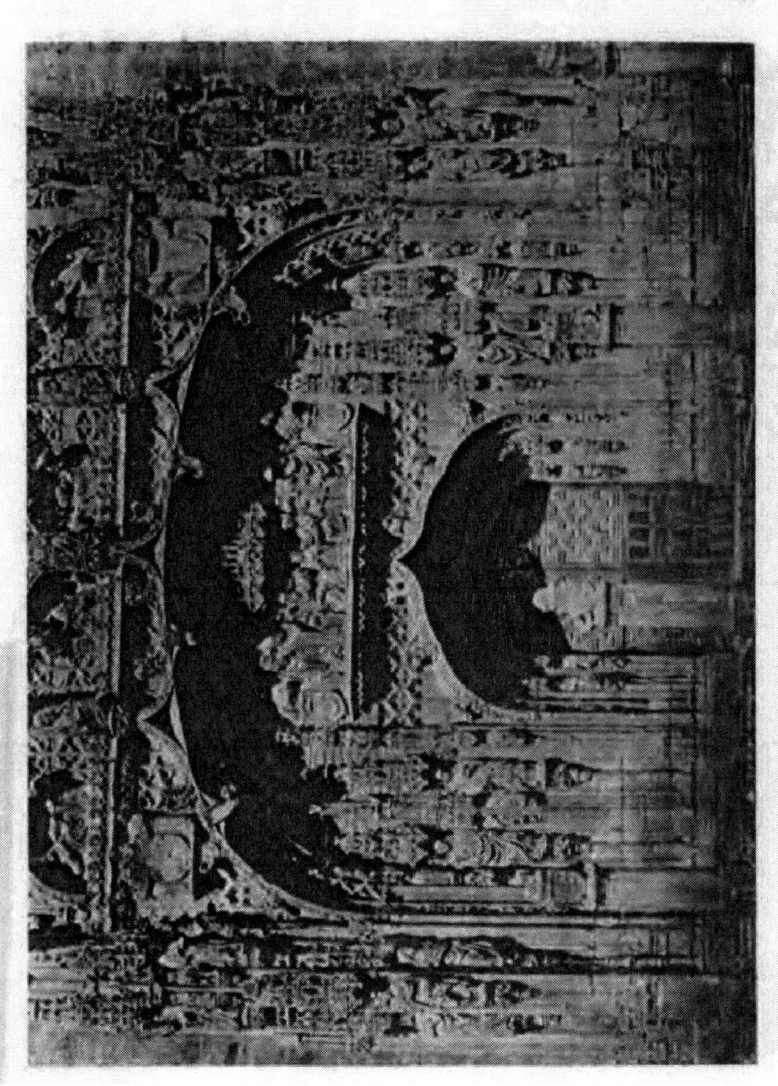

PLATE 41

LOWER CENTRAL PART OF THE FAÇADE OF ST. PABLO

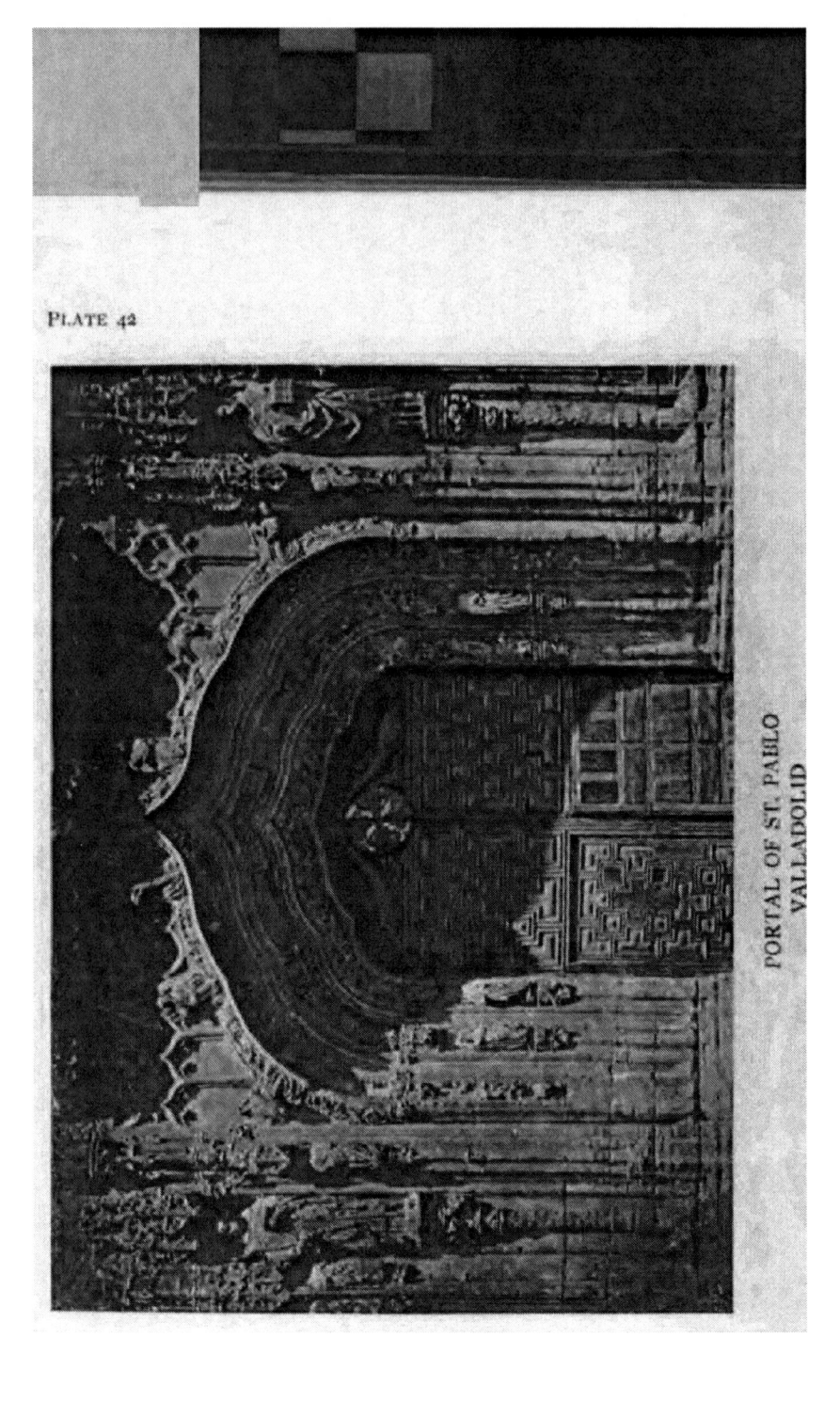

PLATE 42

PORTAL OF ST. PABLO
VALLADOLID

PLATE 43

DETAIL OF THE RIGHT-HAND SIDE OF THE
PORCH OF ST. PABLO
VALLADOLID

PLATE 44

PLATE 45

GENERAL VIEW
OVIEDO

PLATE 46

TOWER OF THE CATHEDRAL
OVIEDO

PLATE 47

PLATE 48

PLATE 49

CATHEDRAL. VIEW OF THE INTERIOR
OVIEDO

PLATE 50

CATHEDRAL. THE RETABLO
OVIEDO

PLATE 51

LA CAMARA SANTA; OR PRIMITIVE CHAPEL OF SAN MIGUEL, WHERE ARE
PRESERVED THE RELICS SAVED BY PELAYO FROM THE
HANDS OF THE MOORS

PLATE 52

COFFIN IN OVIEDO CATHEDRAL, AND DETAILS OF THE
SEPULCHRE FROM COVADONGA
OVIEDO

PLATE 53

OLD TOWER OF THE CATHEDRAL
OVIEDO

PLATE 50

CATHEDRAL. THE RETABLO
OVIEDO

PLATE 55

SECTION, PLAN, AND DETAILS OF THE CAMARA SANTA
IN THE CATHEDRAL
OVIEDO.

PLATE 56

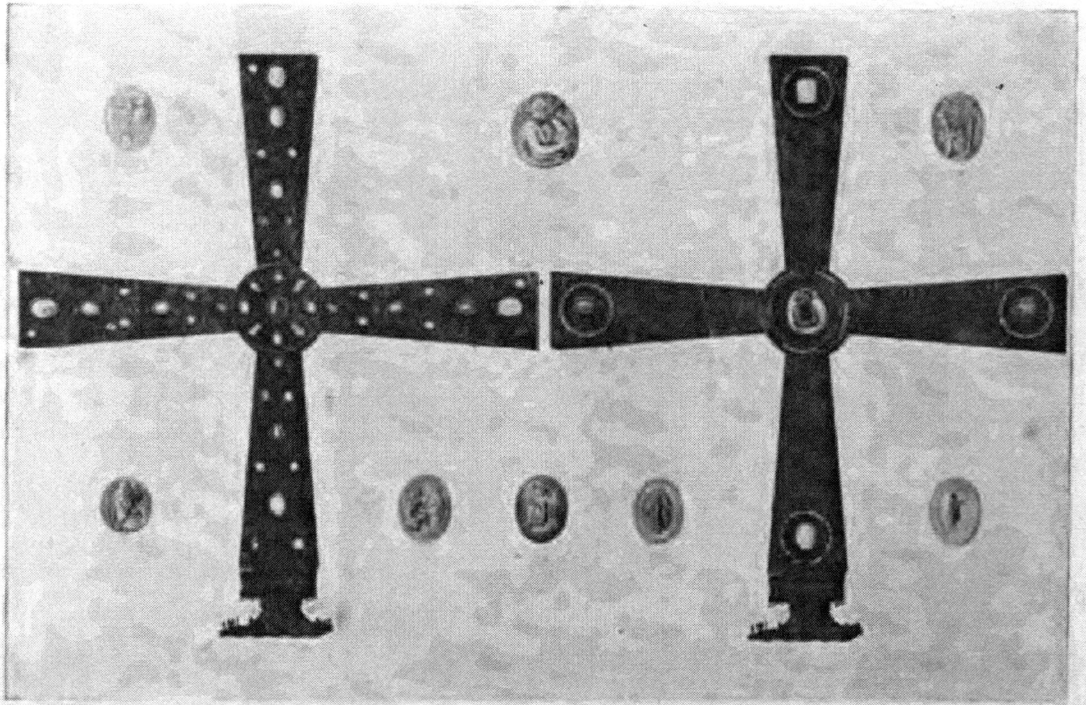

CATHEDRAL. CROSS OF THE ANGELS, IN THE CAMARA SANTA
OVIEDO

PLATE 57

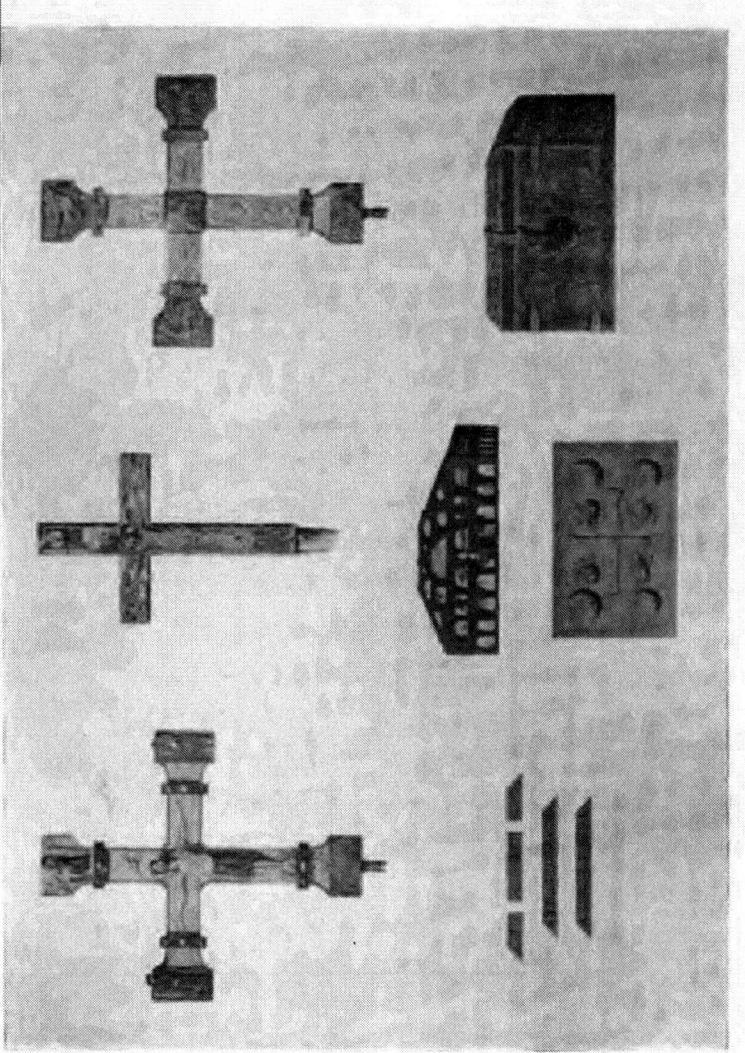

CROSSES AND CASKETS OF THE ASTURIAS
OVIEDO

PLATE 58

CATHEDRAL. CROSS OF VICTORY, OR OF PELAYO, IN THE CAMARA SANTA
OVIEDO

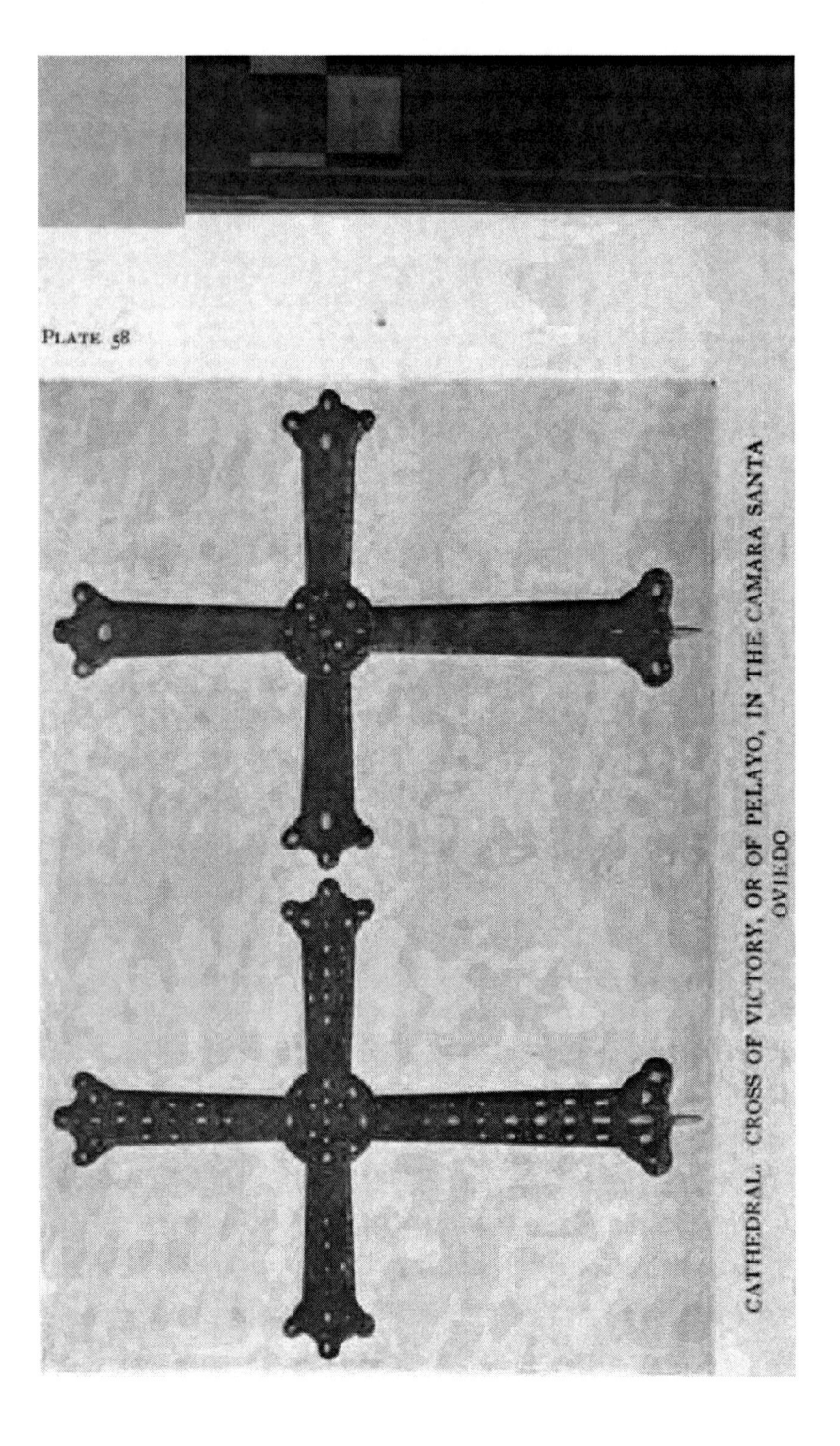

PLATE 59

CAPITAL, REPRESENTING THE DEATH OF FAVILA
THE FATHER OF PELAYA
OVIEDO

PLATE 60

SANTA MARIA DE NARANCO
OVIEDO

PLATE 61

THE PARISH CHURCH OF SANTA MARIA DE NARANCO
OVIEDO

PLATE 62

CHURCH OF SAN MIGUEL DE LINEO

PLATE 63

PARISH CHURCH OF SAN JUAN DE PRIORIO
OVIEDO

PLATE 64

CHURCH OF SAN JUAN DE PRIORIO
OVIEDO

PLATE 65

PORTALS, TOWER, AND DETAILS OF THE CHURCHES OF
ST. CLARA, ST. JOHN, AND OUR LADY DE LA VEGA, THE
LAST-NAMED FOUNDED IN THE TWELFTH CENTURY

COFFIN IN OVIEDO CATHEDRAL, AND DETAILS OF THE
SEPULCHRE FROM COVADONGA
OVIEDO

PLATE 67

PLAN AND DETAILS OF SANTA MARIA DE VALDEDIOS
(CONCEJO DE VILLAVICIOSA)
PROVINCE OF OVIEDO

PLATE 68

PLAN, PRINCIPAL ENTRANCE, AND DETAILS OF THE
CHURCH OF SAN JUAN DE AMANDI (CONCEJO DE
VILLAVICIOSA)
PROVINCE OF OVIEDO

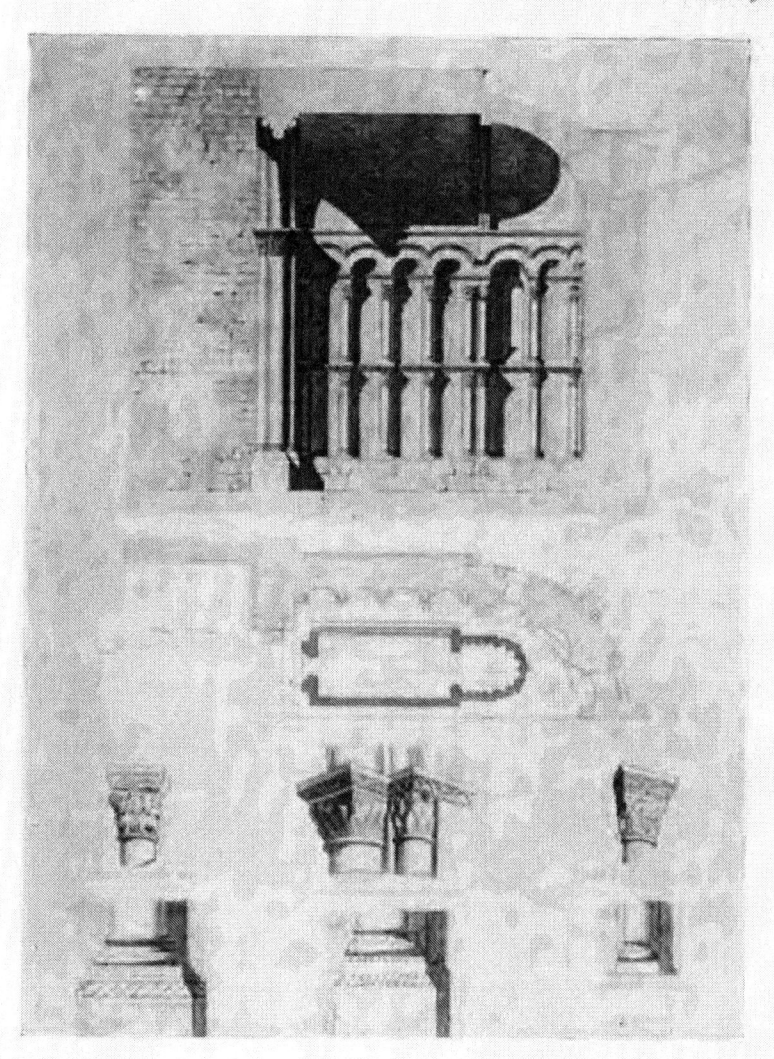

PLATE 69

PLAN, LONGITUDINAL SECTION, AND DETAILS OF THE
PARISH CHURCH OF SAN JUAN DE AMANDI (CONCEJO
DE VILLAVICIOSA)
PROVINCE OF OVIEDO

PLATE 70

PLAN, PORCH, AND DETAILS OF THE PARISH CHURCH OF
VILLAVICIOSA (CONCEJO DE VILLAVICIOSA)
PROVINCE OF OVIEDO

PLATE 71

FRONT, LONGITUDINAL SECTION, AND DETAILS OF THE
PARISH CHURCH OF VILLAVICIOSA (CONCEJO DE
VILLAVICIOSA)
PROVINCE OF OVIEDO

PLATE 72

PLATE 73

TRANSVERSE SECTION AND WINDOWS OF THE CHURCH
OF SAN SALVADOR DE VALDEDIOS (CONCEJO DE
VILLAVICIOSA)
PROVINCE OF OVIEDO

PLATE 74

PLANS, SECTIONS, AND DETAILS OF THE PAROCHIAL
CHURCHES OF PRIESCA AND FUENTES (CONCEJO

PLATE 7

DETAILS OF CHURCH OF SANTA MARIA DE VILLAMAYOR
(CONCEJO DEL INFIESTO)
PROVINCE OF OVIEDO

PLATE 76

DETAILS OF SANTA MARÍA DE VILLAMAYOR (CONCEJO DE INFIESTO)
PROVINCE OF OVIEDO

PLATE 77

PLAN, SECTIONS, AND DETAILS OF SAN ADRIAN DE

PLATE 78

DETAILS OF HERMITAGE OF SANTA CRISTINA (CONCEJO
DE LA POLA DE LENA)
PROVINCE OF OVIEDO

PLATE 7

DETAILS OF SEPULCHRES IN THE CLOISTERS OF THE
COLLEGIATE CHURCH OF COVADONGA (CONCEJO DE
CANGAS DE ONIS)
PROVINCE OF OVIEDO

PLATE 80

PLATE 81

DETAILS OF PAROCHIAL CHURCH OF UJO
(CONCEJO DE MIERES)
OVIEDO

PLATE 82

GENERAL VIEW OF SEGOVIA FROM THE NIEVAS

PLATE 83

GENERAL VIEW OF SEGOVIA

PLATE 84

THE ROMAN AQUEDUCT

PLATE 85

THE ALCAZAR AND CATHEDRAL FROM THE FUENCISLA
SEGOVIA

PLATE 86

GENERAL VIEW FROM THE NIEVAS
SEGOVIA

PLATE 87

OLD HOUSES IN THE PLAZA MAYOR
SEGOVIA

PLATE 88

VIEW OF THE WALLS
SEGOVIA

PLATE 89

AQUEDUCT OVER THE RIVER CASTILLA
SEGOVIA

PLATE 90

THE CATHEDRAL FROM THE HOYOS HILL

PLATE 91

VIEW OF THE CATHEDRAL FROM THE SQUARE
SEGOVIA

PLATE 92

VIEW OF THE CATHEDRAL FROM THE SQUARE
SEGOVIA

PLATE 93

CASA DE LOS PICOS
SEGOVIA

PLATE 94

CHURCH OF SANTA CRUZ

PLATE 95

PORCH OF THE CHURCH OF SANTA CRUZ
SEGOVIA

PLATE 96

CHURCH OF SANTA CRUZ
SEGOVIA

PLATE 97

VIEW OF THE MINT AND THE PARRAL
SEGOVIA

PLATE 98.

PLATE 99

CLOISTERS OF THE PARRAL
SEGOVIA

PLATE 108

GENERAL VIEW OF TURÉGANO

PLATE 101

TURÉGANO CASTLE
PROVINCE OF SEGOVIA

PLATE 102

GENERAL VIEW OF COCA CASTLE

PLATE 103

ANOTHER VIEW OF COCA CASTLE
PROVINCE OF SEGOVIA

PLATE 104

ST. ANDREW'S GATE

PLATE 105

THE ARCH OF THE FUENCISLA
SEGOVIA

PLATE 106

GATE OF SANTIAGO
SEGOVIA

PLATE 107

THE ALCAZAR BEFORE THE FIRE IN 1862
SEGOVIA

PLATE 108

THE ALCAZAR FROM THE HOYOS HILL
SEGOVIA

PLATE 109

VIEW OF THE ALCAZAR
SEGOVIA

PLATE 110

THE ALCAZAR FROM THE CAVES
SEGOVIA

PLATE III

FAÇADE OF THE ALCAZAR BEFORE THE FIRE IN 1862
SEGOVIA

PLATE 112

SEPULCHRES OF THE FAMILY OF THE MARQUESES DE VILLENA IN THE CHURCH OF THE PARRAL

PLATE 113

CHURCH OF ST. NICHOLAS
SEGOVIA

PLATE 114

GENERAL VIEW OF THE CHURCH OF VERA CRUZ

PLATE 115

PORCH OF THE CHURCH OF VERA CRUZ

PLATE 116

COURTYARD OF THE MARQUIS OF ARCOS' HOUSE
SEGOVIA

PLATE 117

FAÇADE OF ST. JOHN
SEGOVIA

PLATE 118

CHURCH OF ST. JOHN. FROM THE EAST
SEGOVIA

PLATE 119

SAN JUAN DE LOS CABALLEROS
SEGOVIA

PLATE 120

CHURCH OF ST. MARTIN
SEGOVIA

PLATE 121

PORCH OF ST. MARTIN

PLATE 122

PARISH CHURCH OF ST. MARTIN
SEGOVIA

PLATE 123

ARCH OF THE PORTICO, CORNICE AND CAPITALS OF THE
PORTICO OF THE PARISH CHURCH OF ST. MARTIN

PLATE 124

GENERAL VIEW OF ST. STEPHEN

PLATE 125

PORTICO OF ST. STEPHEN
SEGOVIA

PLATE 126

PLATE 127

CHURCH OF SAN LORENZO
SEGOVIA

PLATE 128

PLATE 129

LATERAL FAÇADE OF THE CHURCH OF SAN LORENZO
SEGOVIA

PLATE 130

THE CHURCH OF SAN LORENZO, WITH DETAILS OF CAPITALS

PLATE 131

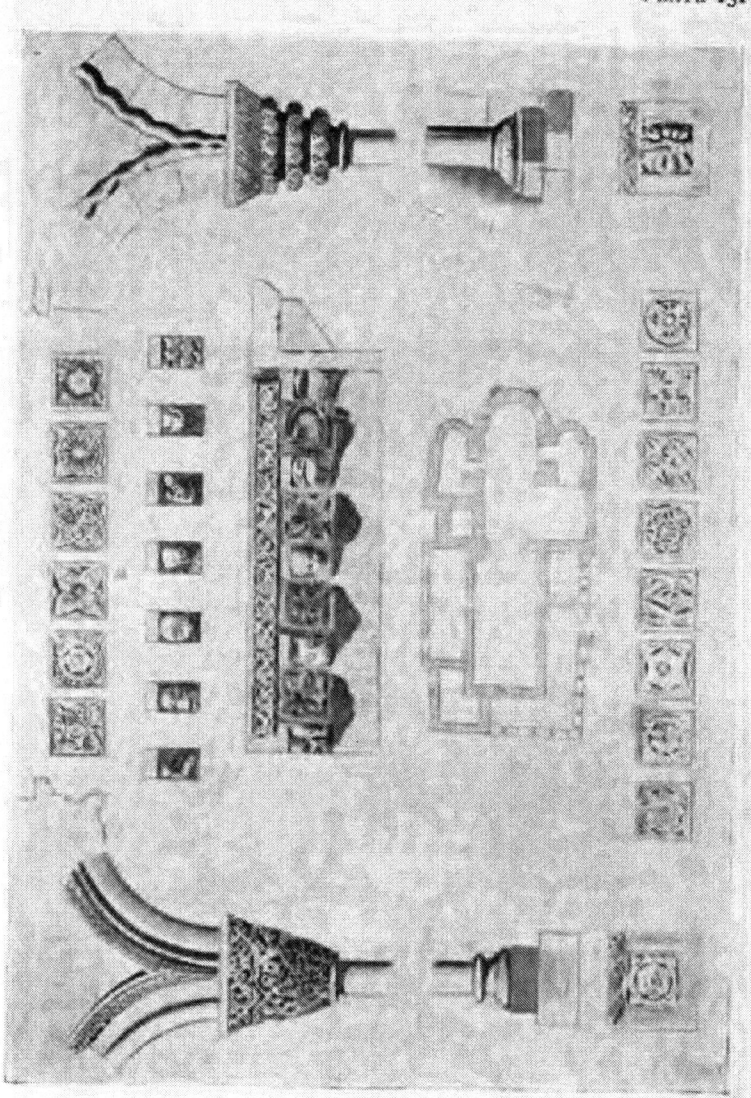

PLAN AND DETAILS OF THE CHURCH OF SAN LORENZO
SEGOVIA

PLATE 133

PLATE 134

ARCHES AND EAVES OF SAN MILLÁN
SEGOVIA

PLATE 135

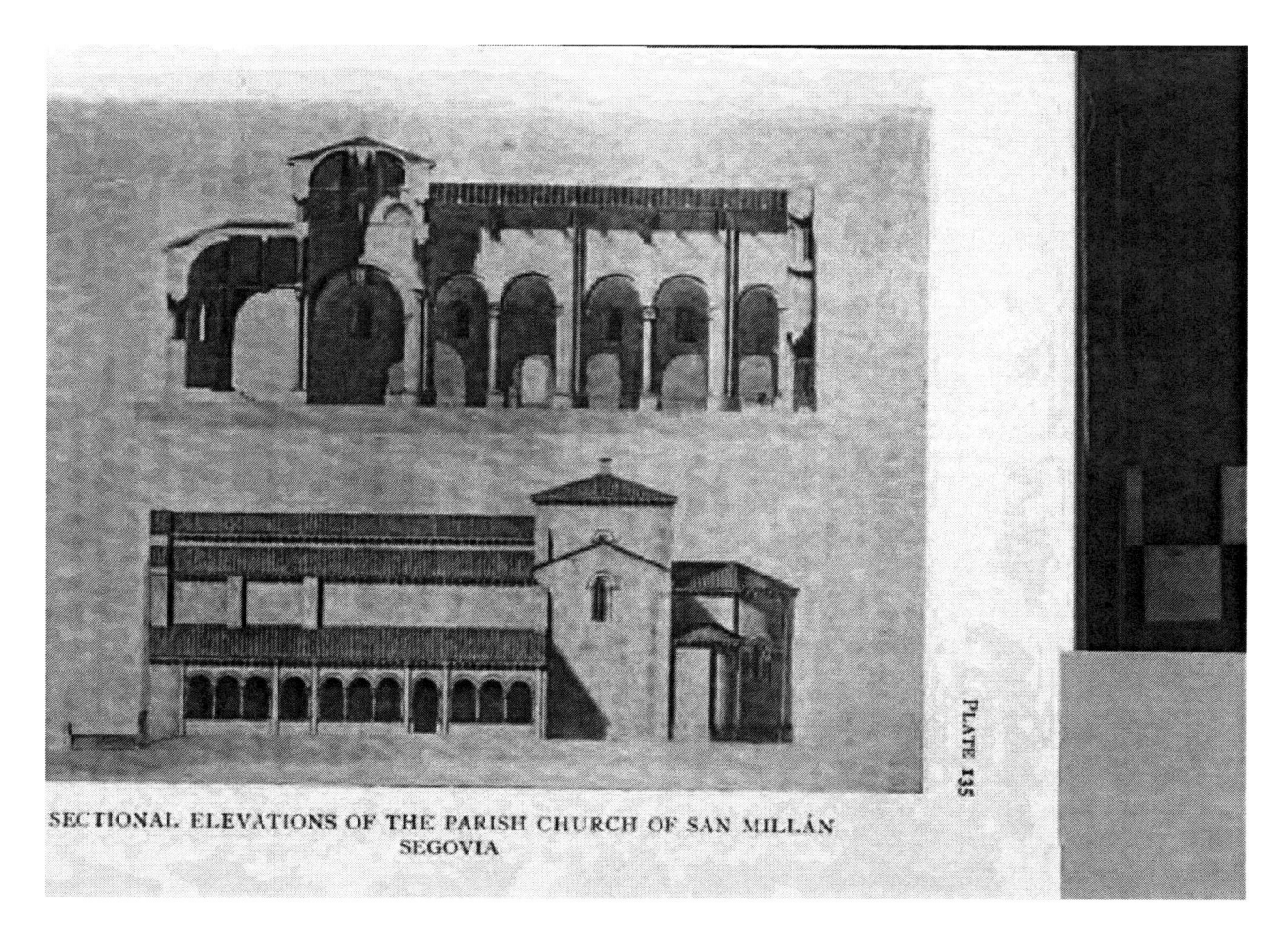

SECTIONAL ELEVATIONS OF THE PARISH CHURCH OF SAN MILLÁN
SEGOVIA

PLATE 136

PLAN, AND DETAILS OF THE PARISH CHURCH OF SAN MILLÁN
SEGOVIA

PLATE 137

DETAILS OF THE PARISH CHURCH OF SAN MILLÁN
SEGOVIA

PLATE 138

DETAILS OF THE PARISH CHURCH OF SAN MILLÁN
SEGOVIA

PLATE 139

PLAN, AND DETAILS OF THE CHURCH OF THE CONVENT
OF CORPUS CHRISTI
SEGOVIA

PLATE 140

INTERIOR OF THE CONVENT OF SANTO DOMINGO AND TOWERS
SEGOVIA

PLATE 141

PAINTED SOCLES IN THE INTERIOR OF THE TOWER OF SANTO DOMINGO, COMMONLY CALLED THE TOWER OF HERCULES
SEGOVIA

PLATE 142

FAÇADE OF THE CONVENT OF OUR LADY DE LA SIERRA
SEGOVIA

PLATE 143

RUINS OF THE CHAPEL OF THE CONVENT OF
OUR LADY DE LA SIERRA
SEGOVIA

PLATE 144

INTERIOR OF THE RUINED CONVENT OF
OUR LADY DE LA SIERRA

PORCH OF THE CONVENT OF OUR LADY DE LA SIERRA
SEGOVIA

PLATE 146

GENERAL VIEW OF THE ROMAN AQUEDUCT

PLATE 147

THE ROMAN AQUEDUCT
SEGOVIA

PLATE 148

THE ROMAN AQUEDUCT

PLATE 149

THE ROMAN AQUEDUCT
SEGOVIA

PLATE 150

THE ROMAN AQUEDUCT

PLATE 151

THE ROMAN AQUEDUCT
SEGOVIA

PLATE 152

THE ROMAN AQUEDUCT
SEGOVIA

PLATE 153

A DANCE IN THE PLAZA DEL PUEBLO DE NIEVA, SEGOVIA. BY A. GARCIA MENCIA. (No. 181, EXHIBITION OF 1871)

PLATE 155

GROUP OF PEASANTS OF THE PROVINCE; SEGOVIA

PLATE 156

PEASANTS OF THE PROVINCE
SEGOVIA

PLATE 157

PEASANTS OF THE PROVINCE
SEGOVIA

PLATE 158

PEASANTS OF THE PROVINCE

PLATE 159

PEASANTS OF THE PROVINCE
SEGOVIA

PLATE 160

PEASANTS OF THE PROVINCE
SEGOVIA

PLATE 161

PEASANTS OF THE PROVINCE
SEGOVIA

PLATE 162

PEASANTS OF THE PROVINCE
SEGOVIA

PLATE 163

PEASANTS OF THE PROVINCE
SEGOVIA

PLATE 164

PLATE 165

PEASANTS OF THE PROVINCE
SEGOVIA

PLATE 167

VIEW OF ZAMORA

PLATE 169

STONE BRIDGE OVER THE DUERO

PLATE 170

BRIDGE OVER THE DUERO
ZAMORA

PLATE 171

VIEW OF THE CATHEDRAL, ZAMORA

PLATE 172

FAÇADE OF THE CATHEDRAL, ZAMORA

PLATE 173

CATHEDRAL. GATE OF THE BISHOP
ZAMORA

PLATE 175

CATHEDRAL. GATE OF THE BISHOP

PLATE 176

CATHEDRAL. GATE OF THE BISHOP

PLATE 177

ANCIENT CISTERCIAN MONASTERY OF MORERUELA
PROVINCE OF ZAMORA

PLATE 178

ANCIENT CISTERCIAN MONASTERY OF MORERUELA
PROVINCE OF ZAMORA

PLATE 179

ANCIENT CISTERCIAN MONASTERY OF MORERUELA
DETAIL OF THE INTERIOR
PROVINCE OF ZAMORA

PLATE 180

ANCIENT CISTERCIAN MONASTERY OF MORERUELA.
DETAIL OF THE INTERIOR
PROVINCE OF ZAMORA

PLATE 181

ANCIENT CISTERCIAN MONASTERY OF
MORERUELA. CHANCEL
PROVINCE OF ZAMORA

PLATE 182

ANCIENT CISTERCIAN MONASTERY OF MOREROELA. EXAMPLE OF THE VAULTING

PLATE 183

ANCIENT CISTERCIAN MONASTERY OF MORERUELA. INTERIOR
PROVINCE OF ZAMORA

PLATE 184

ANCIENT CISTERCIAN MONASTERY OF MORERUELA. TRANSEPT AND NAVE
PROVINCE OF ZAMORA

ANCIENT CISTERCIAN MONASTERY OF MORERUELA
DETAIL OF A WINDOW DEEPLY RECESSED
PROVINCE OF ZAMORA

PLATE 186

ANCIENT CISTERCIAN MONASTERY OF MORERUELA
TRANSEPT PORCH
PROVINCE OF ZAMORA

PLATE 187

SANTA MARIA LA NUEVA. DETAIL OF THE EXTERIOR
PROVINCE OF ZAMORA

PLATE 190

CHURCH OF THE MAGDALEN

PLATE 191

PRINCIPAL DOOR OF THE CHURCH OF THE MAGDALEN
ZAMORA

PLATE 192

PLAN AND SECTIONS OF THE PARISH CHURCH
OF ST. PETER

PLATE 193

DETAILS OF THE PARISH CHURCH OF ST. PETER (NAVE)
ZAMORA

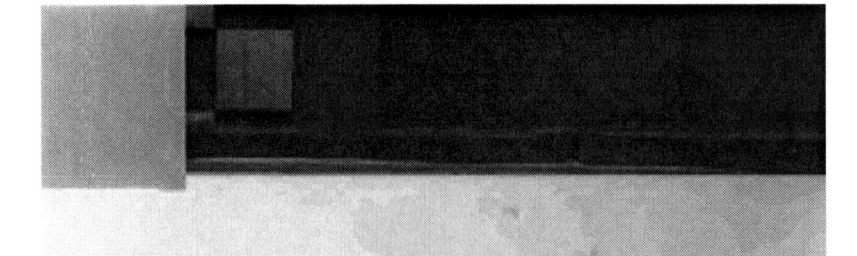

PLATE 192

PLAN AND SECTIONS OF THE PARISH CHURCH
OF ST. PETER

PLATE 193

DETAILS OF THE PARISH CHURCH OF ST. PETER (NAVE)
ZAMORA

PLATE 194

HOUSE OF THE CID

PLATE 195

TAPESTRY OF THE BEGINNING OF THE FIFTEENTH CENTURY
ZAMORA

PLATE 196

DECORATIVE PAINTING IN THE TOWN HALL. BY RAMON
PEDRO Y PEDRET

PLATE 197

PAINTING IN THE TOWN HALL
BY RAMON PEDRO Y PEDRET
ZAMORA

PLATE 198

PAINTING ON THE UPPER PART OF THE CENTRE HALL
OF THE TOWN HALL. BY RAMON PEDRO Y PEDRET
ZAMORA

PLATE 199

PAINTING ON THE LOWER PART OF THE CENTRE HALL OF
THE TOWN HALL. BY RAMON PEDRO Y PEDRET
ZAMORA

PLATE 200

THE ROYAL ESCUTCHEON. DECORATIVE PAINTING IN THE
TOWN HALL. BY RAMON PEDRO Y PEDRET
ZAMORA

PLATE 201

ST. FERDINAND AND KING JOHN II. DECORATIVE PAINTING
IN THE TOWN HALL. BY RAMON PEDRO Y PEDRET
ZAMORA

PLATE 202

THE ARMS OF THE TOWN. BY RAMON PEDRO Y PEDRET
ZAMORA

PLATE 203

QUEEN URRACA AND ARIAS GONZALO. DECORATIVE PAINTING
IN THE TOWN HALL. BY RAMON PEDRO Y PEDRET
ZAMORA

PLATE 204

TROPHIES OF ARMS AND ARMOUR IN THE TOWN HALL

PLATE 205

THE HOUSE OF THE MOMOS
ZAMORA

PLATE 208

EARTHWORKS OF THE ANCIENT CITY OF TORO

PLATE 209

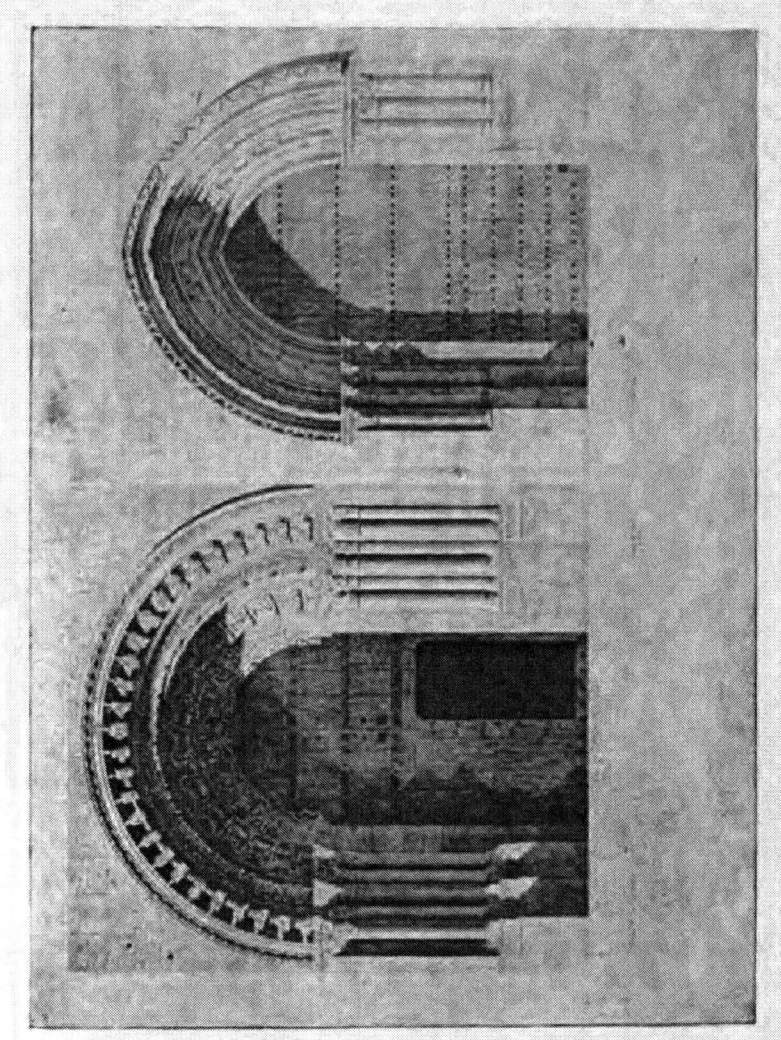

NORTH AND CENTRE GATES OF THE COLLEGIATE CHURCH OF TORO

PLATE 210

PLAN, EXTERIOR VIEW, AND DETAILS OF THE COLLEGIATE CHURCH OF TORO

PLATE 311

GROUP OF PEASANTS OF THE VILLAGE OF BERMIGO DE SAYAGO
PROVINCE OF ZAMORA

PLATE 212

GROUP OF PEASANTS OF THE VILLAGE OF CARBAJALES
PROVINCE OF ZAMORA

PLATE 213

PEASANTS OF THE VILLAGE OF BERMIGO DE SAYAGO
PROVINCE OF ZAMORA

PLATE 218

GATE OF SAN VICENTE

PLATE 219

GATE OF SAN VICENTE
AVILA

PLATE 220

GATE OF SAN VICENTE, ENTRANCE TO AVILA

PLATE 221

GATE OF SAN VICENTE
AVILA

PLATE 222

A STREET IN AVILA

PLATE 223

VIEW OF THE CATHEDRAL, AVILA

PLATE 230

GATE OF SAN VICENTE ENTRANCE TO AVILA

PLATE 225

ENTRANCE TO THE CATHEDRAL
AVILA

PLATE 226

PLAN OF THE CATHEDRAL

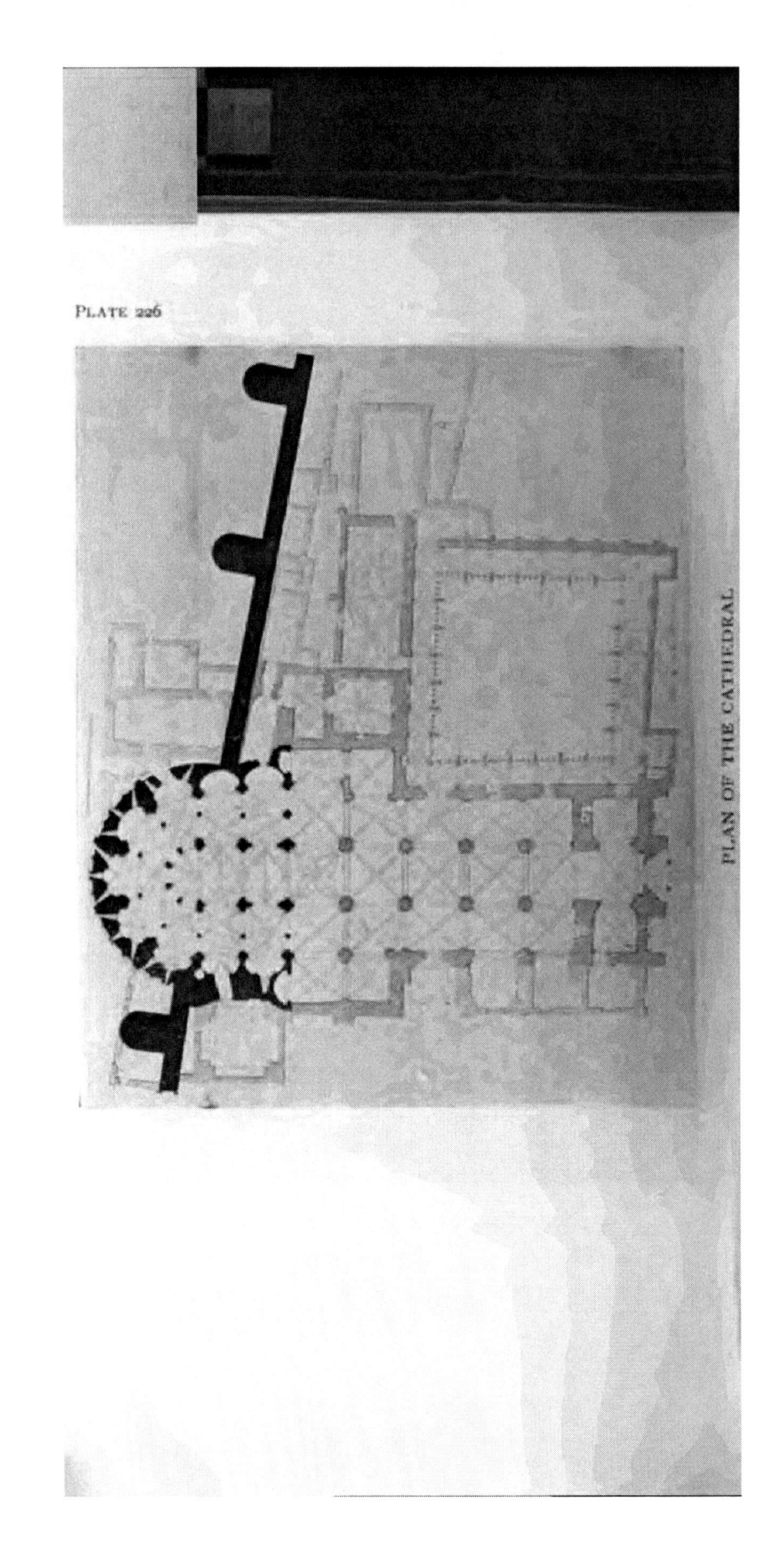

PLATE 227

AVILA CATHEDRAL

PLATE 228

SIDE DOOR OF THE CATHEDRAL

PLATE 229

CATHEDRAL. PULPIT OF REPOUSSÉ IRON WORK
AVILA

PLATE 230

CATHEDRAL. PULPIT OF REPOUSSÉ IRON WORK
AVILA

PLATE 231

CATHEDRAL. PULPIT OF REPOUSSÉ IRON WORK
AVILA

PLATE 232

INTERIOR OF THE CATHEDRAL
AVILA

PLATE 233

CATHEDRAL. DETAIL OF THE INTERIOR
AVILA

CATHEDRAL. PULPIT OF REPOUSSÉ IRON WORK
AVILA

PLATE 236

PLATE 237

CATHEDRAL. DETAIL OF THE CHOIR
AVILA

PLATE 238

CATHEDRAL. DETAIL OF THE CHOIR
AVILA

PLATE 239

CATHEDRAL. ALTAR OF SAN SEGUNDO
AVILA

PLATE 237

CATHEDRAL. DETAIL OF THE CHOIR
AVILA

PLATE 239

CATHEDRAL. ALTAR OF SAN SEGUNDO
AVILA

PLATE 242

CATHEDRAL. TOMB OF EL TESTADO
BISHOP OF AVILA IN 1449
AVILA

PLATE 243

CATHEDRAL. ALTAR BEHIND THE CHOIR
AVILA

PLATE 242

CATHEDRAL. TOMB OF EL TESTADO
BISHOP OF AVILA IN 1449
AVILA

PLATE 243

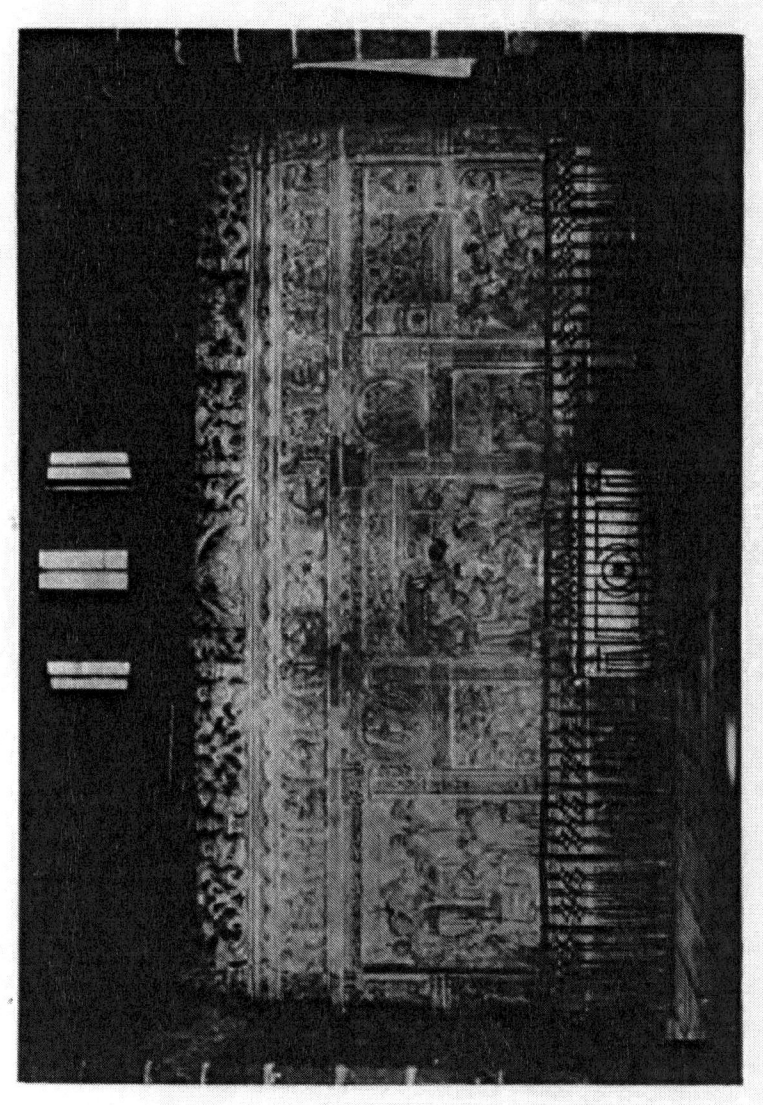

CATHEDRAL. ALTAR BEHIND THE CHOIR
AVILA

PLATE 244

CATHEDRAL. SILVER MONSTRANCE OF JUAN
DE ARFE. SIXTEENTH CENTURY

PLATE 245

CONVENT OF SANTO TOMÁS
SEPULCHRE OF THE INFANTE DON JUAN, SON OF FERDINAND AND ISABELLA
THE MASTERPIECE OF MICER DOMENICO OF FLORENCE
AVILA

PLATE 246

SEPULCHRE OF THE HOLY MARTYRS VICENTE, SABINA AND CRISTINA
AVILA

PLATE 247

INTERIOR OF THE CHAPEL OF SAN BERNARDO
BY P. GONZALVO
AVILA

ENTRANCE TO THE CHURCH OF ST. PETER
AVILA

PLATE 250

PAROCHIAL CHURCH OF ST. PETER

PLATE 251

LONGITUDINAL SECTION AND DETAILS OF THE PARISH CHURCH
OF ST. PETER, AVILA

PLATE 253

BASILICA OF SAN VICENTE BEFORE ITS RESTORATION
AVILA

PLATE 254

BASILICA OF SAN VICENTE BEFORE ITS RESTORATION
AVILA

PLATE 255

BASILICA OF SAN VICENTE. NORTH FAÇADE
AVILA

PLATE 256

BASILICA OF SAN VICENTE. PRINCIPAL FAÇADE
AVILA

PLATE 257

BASILICA OF SAN VICENTE. EASTERN FAÇADE, RESTORED)
AVILA

PLATE 258

PLATE 259

BASILICA OF SAN VICENTE. CENTRAL GATE, RESTORED
AVILA

PLATE 260

BASILICA OF SAN VICENTE. DETAIL OF THE MIDDLE CORNICE, RESTORED

PORTAL OF THE BASILICA OF SAN VICENTE,
SANTAS SABINA AND CRISTINA

PLATE 262

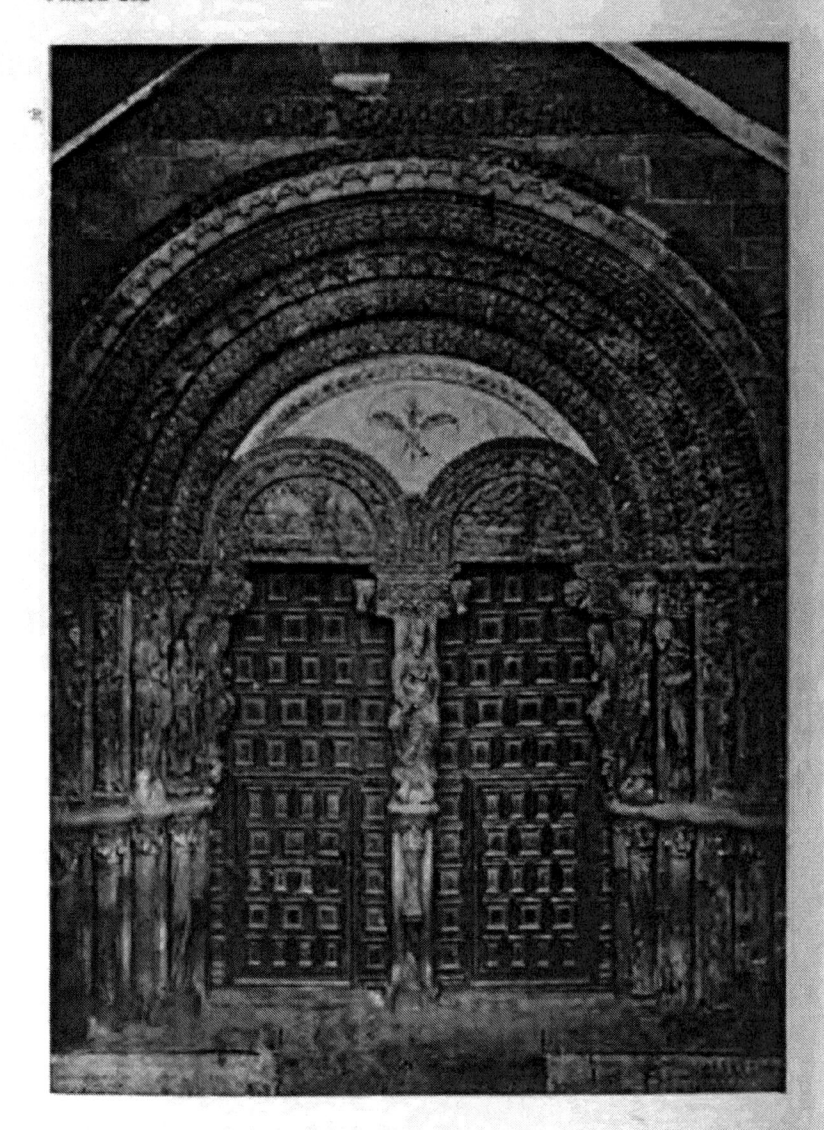

BASILICA OF SAN VICENTE. PRINCIPAL WEST ENTRANCE
AVILA

BASILICA OF SAN VICENTE. PRINCIPAL WEST ENTRANCE
AVILA

PLATE 264

BASILICA OF SAN VICENTE. GENERAL VIEW OF
THE INTERIOR
AVILA

PLATE 265

BASILICA OF SAN VICENTE. SEPULCHRE OF THE
HOLY MARTYRS

PLATE 256

BASILICA OF SAN VICENTE. PRINCIPAL FAÇADE
AVILA

PLATE 257

BASILICA OF SAN VICENTE. EASTERN FAÇADE, RESTORED;

PLATE 258

BASILICA OF SAN VICENTE. FAÇADE

BASILICA OF SAN VICENTE. CENTRAL GATE, RESTORED
AVILA

PLATE 260

BASILICA OF SAN VICENTE. DETAIL OF THE MIDDLE CORNICE, RESTORED
AVILA

PLATE 261

PORTAL OF THE BASILICA OF SAN VICENTE,
SANTAS SABINA AND CRISTINA

PLATE 262

BASILICA OF SAN VICENTE. PRINCIPAL WEST ENTRANCE
AVILA

PLATE 263

BASILICA OF SAN VICENTE. PRINCIPAL WEST ENTRANCE
AVILA

PLATE 264

BASILICA OF SAN VICENTE. GENERAL VIEW OF
THE INTERIOR
AVILA

PLATE 265

BASILICA OF SAN VICENTE. SEPULCHRE OF THE
HOLY MARTYRS

PLATE 258

BASILICA OF SAN VICENTE. FACADE

BASILICA OF SAN VICENTE. CENTRAL GATE, RESTORED
AVILA

PLATE 262

BASILICA OF SAN VICENTE. PRINCIPAL WEST ENTRANCE
AVILA

PLATE 263

BASILICA OF SAN VICENTE. PRINCIPAL WEST ENTRANCE
AVILA

PLATE 264

BASILICA OF SAN VICENTE. GENERAL VIEW OF
THE INTERIOR
AVILA

BASILICA OF SAN VICENTE. SEPULCHRE OF THE
HOLY MARTYRS

PLATE 266

DETAILS OF THE INTERIOR OF THE BASILICA OF
SAN VICENTE
AVILA

PLATE 267

PORCH OF THE CHURCH OF SAN VICENTE
AVILA

PLATE 268

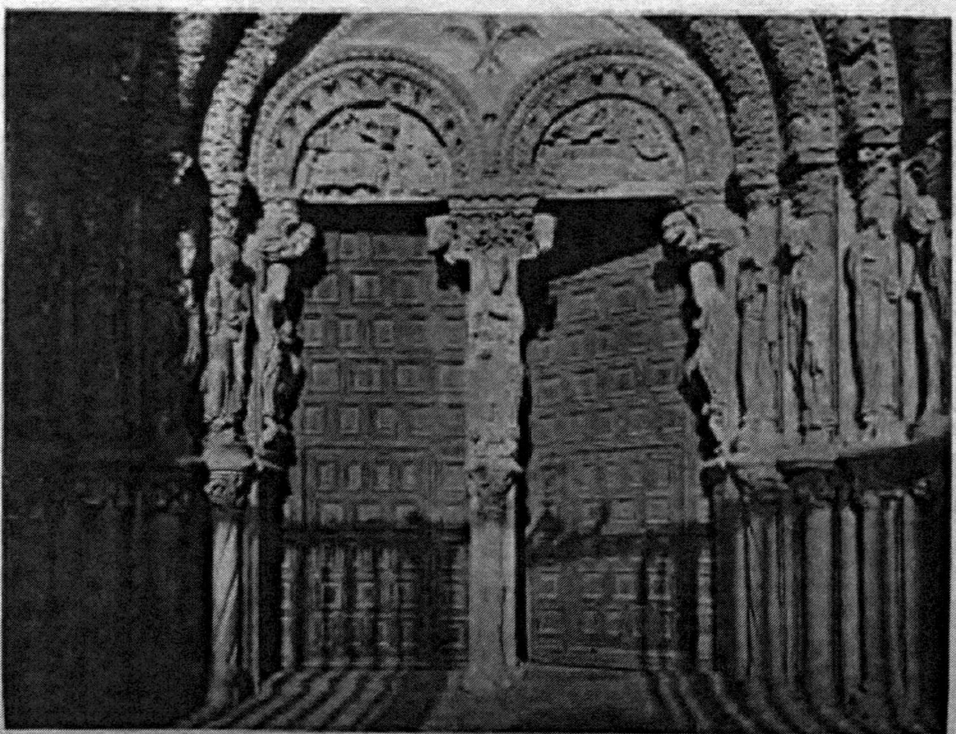

PORCH OF THE CHURCH OF SAN VICENTE. CENTRAL PART

PLATE 269

PORCH OF THE CONVENT OF SANTO TOMÁS
AVILA

PLATE 270

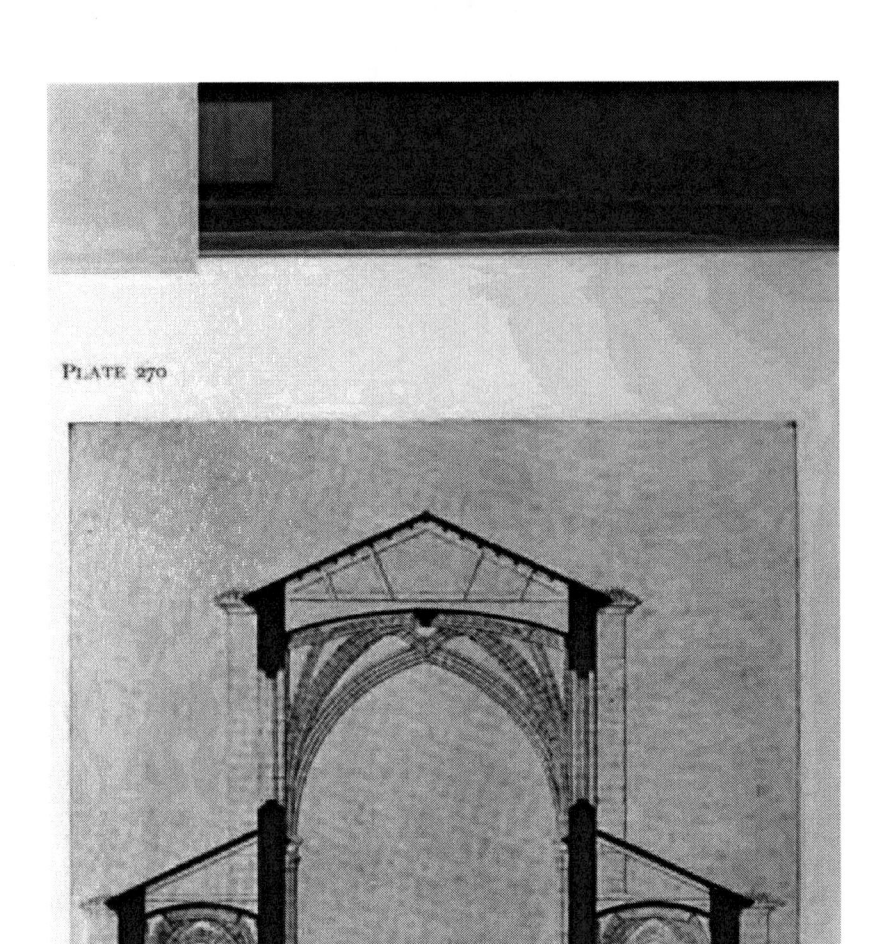

SECTION OF THE CONVENT OF SANTO TOMÁS
AVILA

PLATE 271

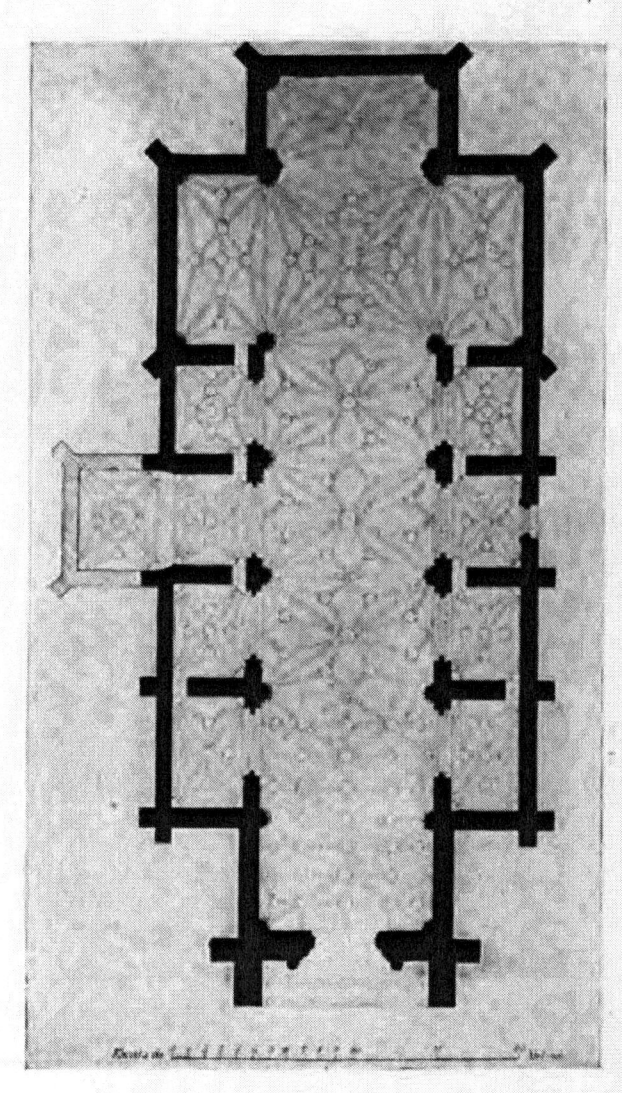

PLAN OF THE CONVENT OF SANTO TOMÁS
AVILA

PLATE 272

GATE OF THE CONVENT OF SANTO TOMÁS

PLATE 273

DOOR OF SANTO TOMÁS
AVILA

PLATE 274

INTERIOR OF SANTO TOMÁS
AVILA

PLATE 275

THE COURT OF SILENCE, IN THE CONVENT OF SANTO TOMÁS
AVILA

PLATE 276

CONVENT OF SANTO TOMÁS. THE COURT OF SILENCE
AVILA

PLATE 277

CONVENT OF SANTO TOMÁS. COURT OF THE KINGS
AVILA

PLATE 278

CONVENT OF SANTO TOMÁS. COURTYARD OF
THE INFIRMARY
AVILA

PLATE 279

PLATE 280

CLOISTERS OF THE CONVENT OF SANTO TOMÁS
ÁVILA

PLATE 281

CLOISTERS OF THE CONVENT OF SANTO TOMÁS
AVILA

PLATE 282

GATE OF THE CLOISTERS IN THE CONVENT OF
SANTO TOMÁS

PLATE 283

CHOIR OF THE CONVENT OF SANTO TOMÁS

PLATE 287

CHURCH OF SAN SEGUNDO. STATUE OF SAN SEGUNDO
BY BERRUGUETE
AVILA

PLATE 289

SANTO TOMÁS. SEPULCHRE OF PRINCE JUAN, ONLY SON OF
FERDINAND AND ISABELLA. AVILA

PLATE 288

CHURCH OF SANTO TOMÁS, SEPULCHRE OF THE INFANTE JUAN, ONLY SON OF

PLATE 289

SANTO TOMÁS, SEPULCHRE OF PRINCE JUAN, ONLY SON OF FERDINAND AND ISABELLA. AVILA

PLATE 290

SANTO TOMÁS. SEPULCHRE OF PRINCE JUAN, ONLY SON OF

PLATE 291

GOTHIC GATE IN RUINS
AVILA

PLATE 292

DOOR OF A PRIVATE HOUSE OPPOSITE THE CATHEDRAL

PLATE 293

CALLE DE PEDRO D'AVILA
VILA

PLATE 296

PORTICO OF THE POLENTINOS' PALACE
AVILA

PLATE 297

CHURCH OF SAN ANDRES AND SAN SEGUNDO
AVILA

PLATE 298

HERMITAGE OF SAN ISIDRO
AVILA

PLATE 297

AN ANDRES AND SAN SEGUNDO

PLATE 306

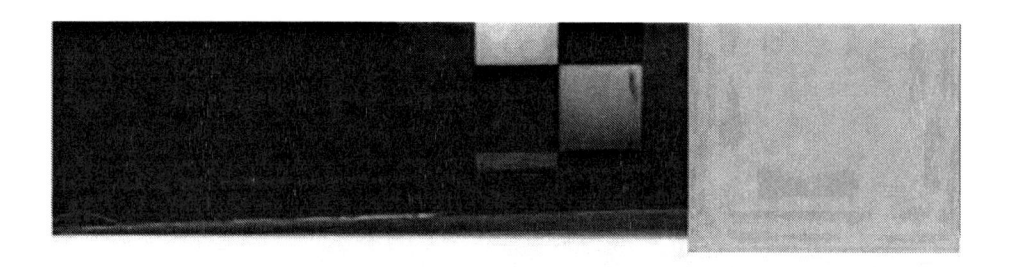

PLATE 301

CASA DE LA BARAGAÑAS

PLATE 302

CASA DE LA TORRE
AVILA

PLATE 303

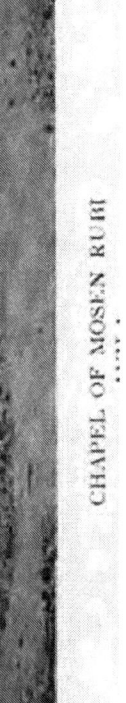

CHAPEL OF MOSEN RUBI

CASA DE LA TORRE
ÁVILA

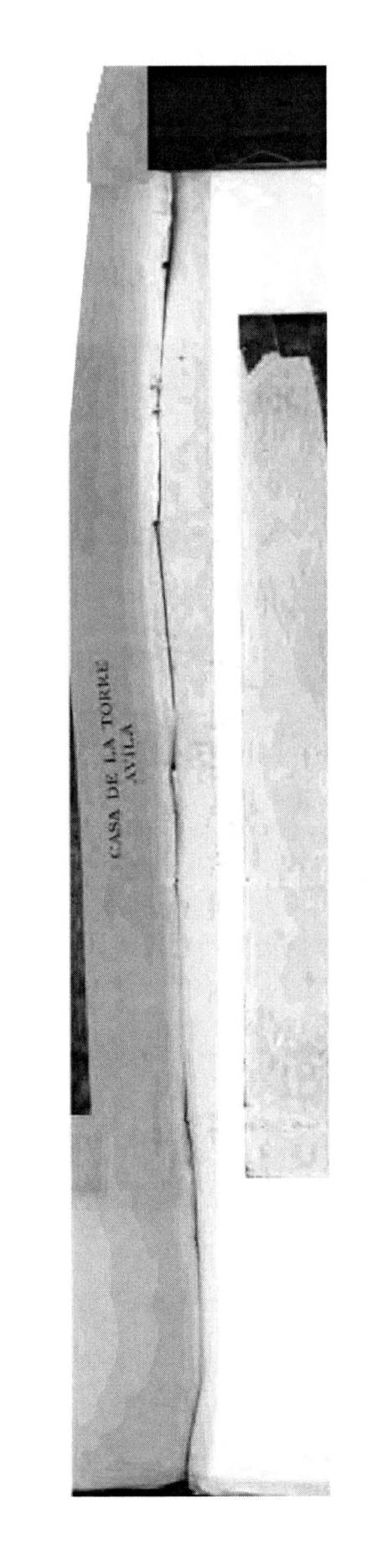

PLATE 305

MINIATURES FROM THE AVILA MISSAL, TWELFTH CENTURY (NATIONAL LIBRARY)

PLATE 306

MINIATURES FROM THE AVILA MISSAL, TWELFTH
CENTURY (NATIONAL LIBRARY)

PLATE 307

DOOR OF SAN FRANCISCO
AVILA

PLATE 308

A ROMAN CAPITAL OF THE CHURCH OF SAN FRANCISCO
AVILA

PLATE 309

LATIN-BYZANTINE FRIEZE IN THE CHURCH OF SAN FRANCISCO
AVILA

PLATE 310

MONASTERY OF SAN PEDRO AT ARENAS

PLATE 311

GENERAL VIEW FROM CABEZO-CORTADO
ZARAGOZA

MONASTERY OF SAN PEDRO AT ARENAS
AVILA

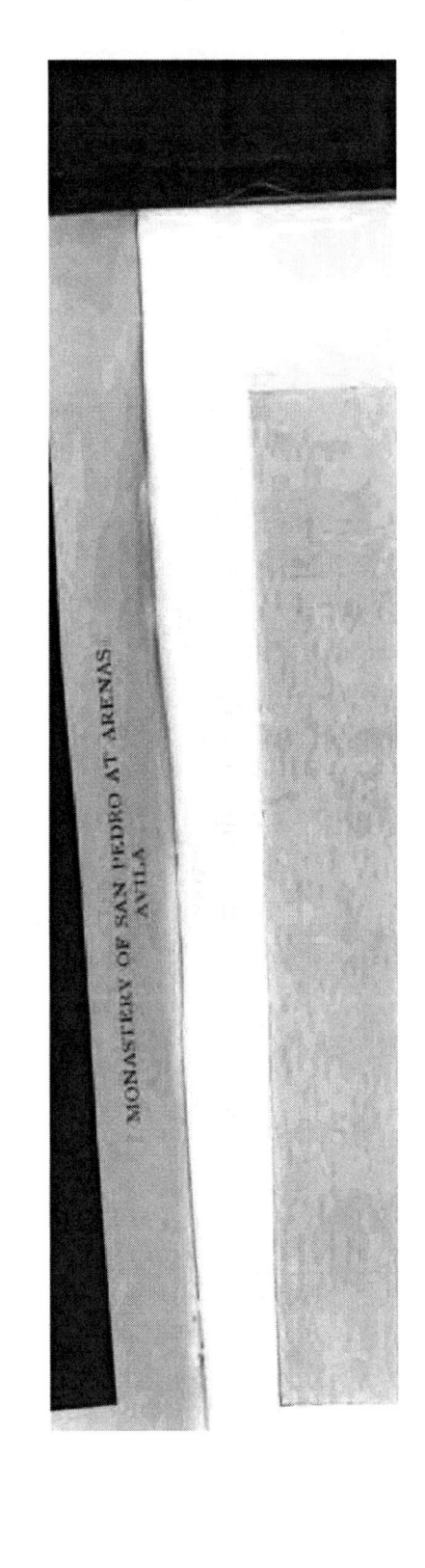

PLATE 313

GENERAL VIEW FROM AL-TABAS
ZARAGOZA

GENERAL VIEW FROM ALTABAS
ZARAGOZA

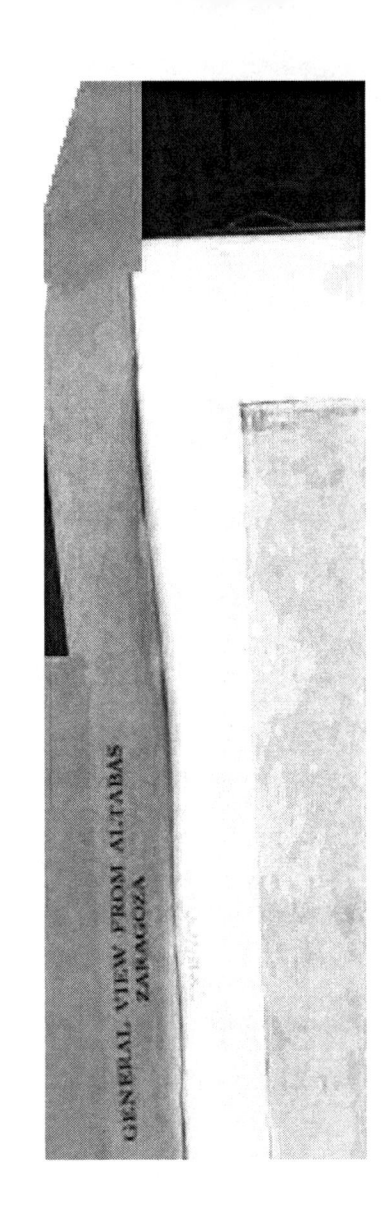

PLATE 315

THE BRIDGE OVER THE EBRO, FROM EL PILAR
ZARAGOZA

PLATE 316

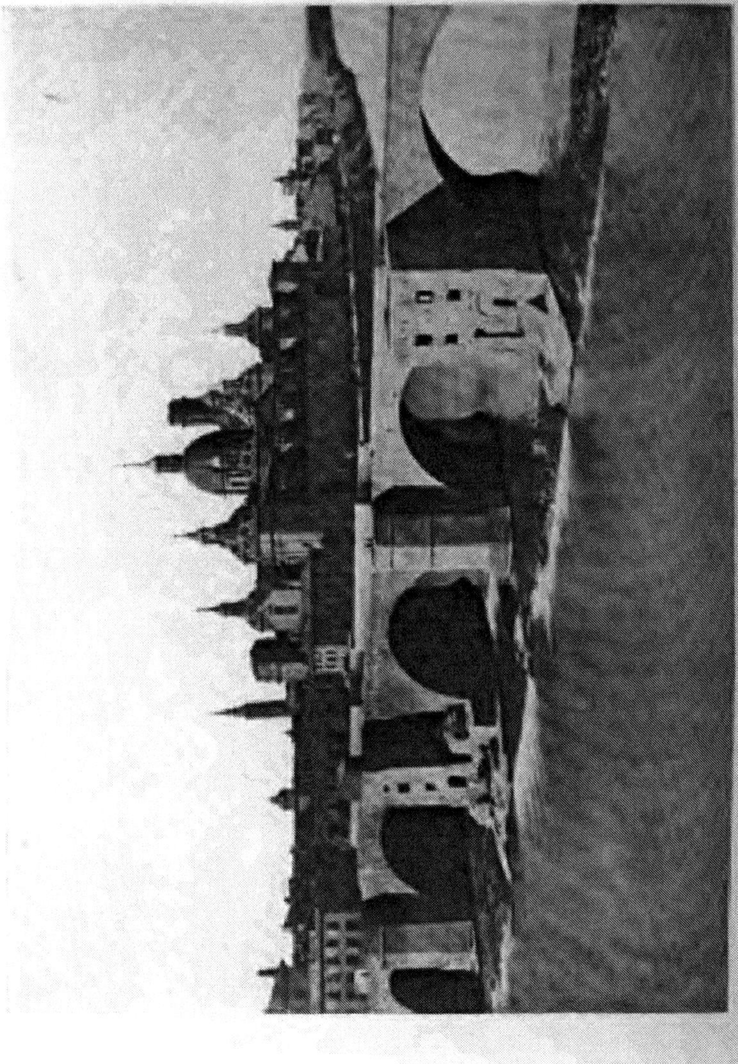

GENERAL VIEW OF FAROGHA

PLATE 317

GENERAL VIEW OF ZARAGOZA

PLATE 318

GENERAL VIEW OF ZARAGOZA

PLATE 317

GENERAL VIEW OF ZARAGOZA

PLATE 320

VIEW OF ZARAGOZA

PLATE 321

CALLE DEL MERCADO
ZARAGOZA

VIEW OF ZARAGOZA

PLATE 323

CATHEDRAL OF LA SEO
ZARAGOZA

PLATE 324

CATHEDRAL OF LA SEO
ZARAGOZA

GLAZED TILES ON THE WALLS OF THE
CATHEDRAL OF LA SEO

PLATE 326

INTERIOR OF THE CATHEDRAL AT SALAMANCA. FROM A PAINTING BY D. ROBERTS.

PLATE 325

...LES ON THE WALLS OF THE
...HEDRAL OF LA SEO
ZARAGOZA

INTERIOR OF THE CATHEDRAL OF LA SEO. FROM A PAINTING BY P. G
(NATIONAL EXHIBITION OF FINE ARTS, 1887). ZARAGOZA

PLATE 329

CHAPEL OF ST. JOHN IN THE CATHEDRAL OF LA SEO

CHAPEL OF GABRIEL DE ZAPORTA IN THE
CATHEDRAL OF LA SEO
ZARAGOZA

PLATE 331

CATHEDRAL OF LA SEO. REJA BRONZE REPOUSSÉ BEFORE THE
CHAPEL OF ZAPORTA, ZARAGOZA

PLATE 332

PLATE 331

CATHEDRAL OF LA SEO. REJA BRONZE REPOUSSÉ BEFORE THE
CHAPEL OF ZAPORTA. ZARAGOZA

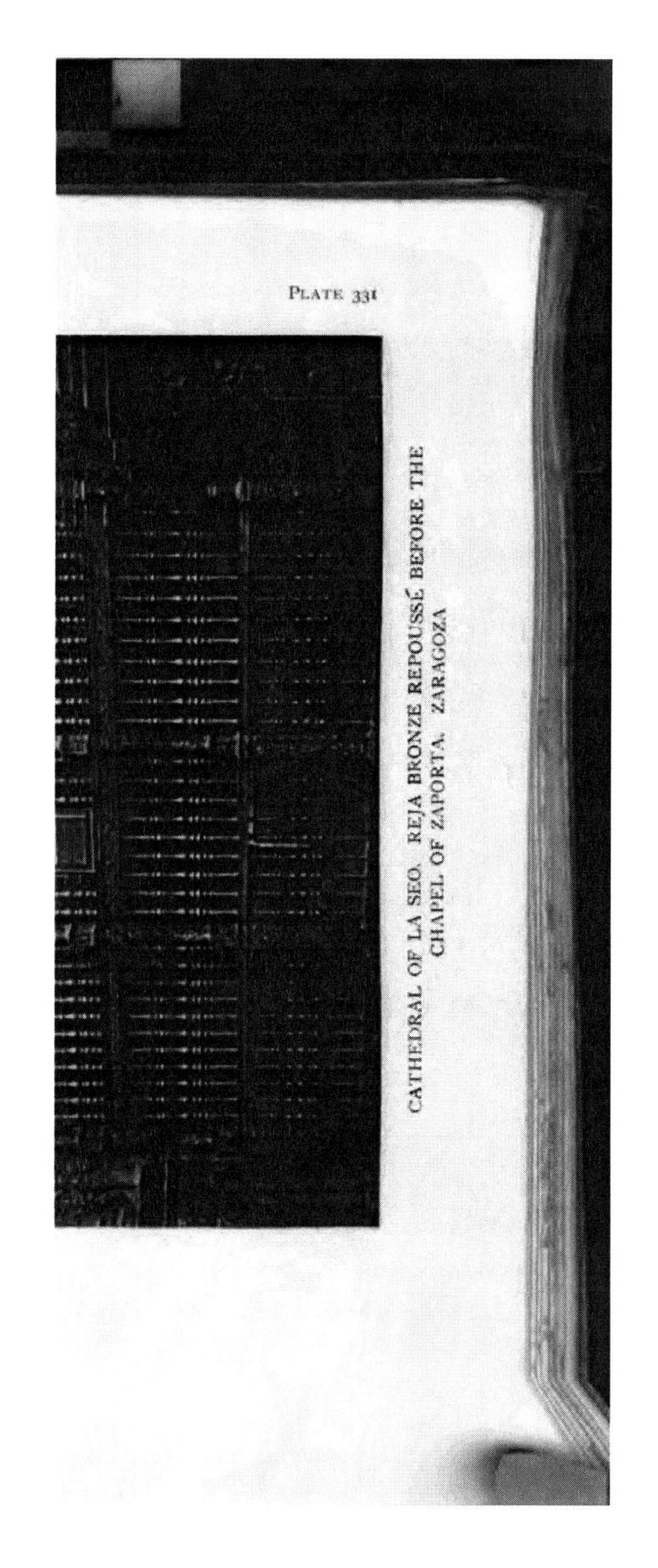

PLATE 334

SILVER MONSTRANCE IN THE CATHEDRAL OF LA
SEO, WEIGHT 200 KILOGRAMMES

PLATE 335

CENSER GIVEN TO THE CATHEDRAL OF LA SEO BY
MOSÉN JUAN DE TORRELLAS AT THE END OF
THE FIFTEENTH CENTURY
ZARAGOZA

PLATE 336

CATHEDRAL OF EL PILAR

PLATE 335

... THE CATHEDRAL OF LA SEO BY
... TORRELLAS AT THE END OF
...IFTEENTH CENTURY
ZARAGOZA

PLATE 338

INTERIOR OF OUR LADY DEL PILAR

PLATE 337

CATHEDRAL OF EL PILAR
ZARAGOZA

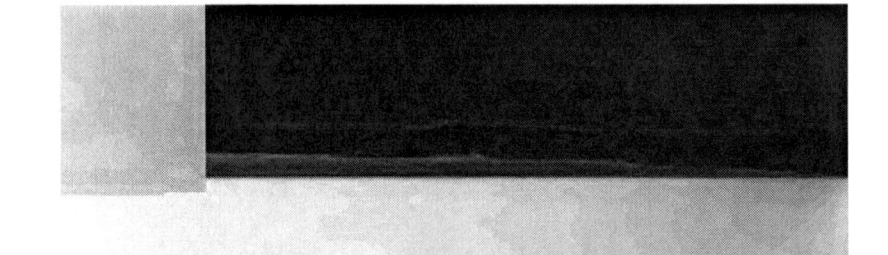

PLATE 340

OUR LADY DEL PILAR. VIEW OF THE CHOIR

PLATE 339

ALTAR IN OUR LADY DEL PILAR
ZARAGOZA

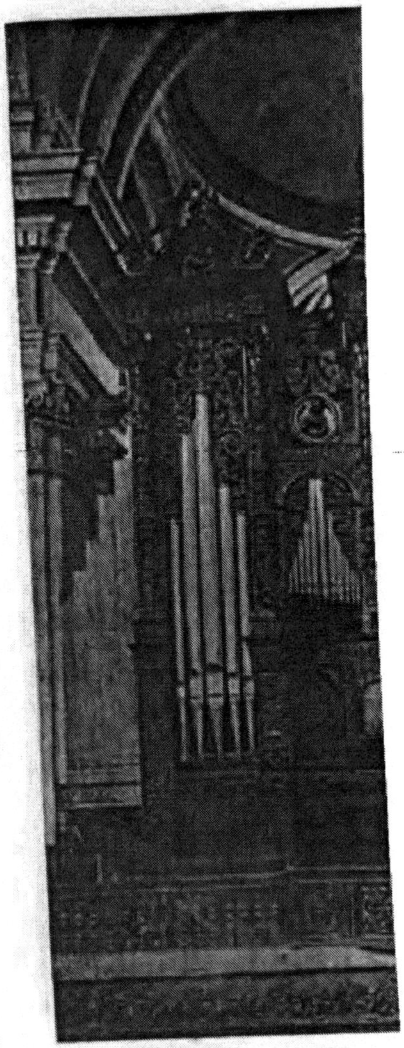

PLATE 343

PLATE 344

PAINTINGS IN THE CUPOLA OF OUR LADY DEL PILAR, ZARAGOZA

PLATE 345

CATHEDRAL OF OUR LADY DEL PILAR. CHOIR STALLS

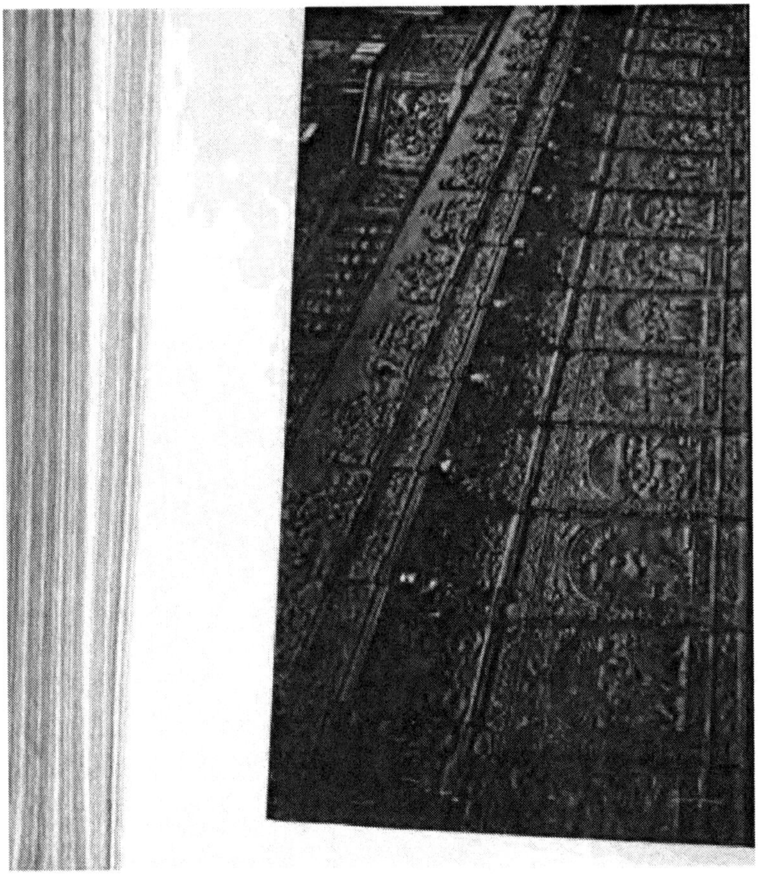

PLATE 347

CATHEDRAL OF OUR LADY DEL PILAR. CHOIR STALLS
ZARAGOZA

CATHEDRAL OF OUR LADY DEL PILAR. CHOIR STALLS
ZARAGOZA

PLATE 349

OUR LADY DEL PILAR
ZARAGOZA

PLATE 350

SILVER SALVER IN THE CATHEDRAL OF EL PILAR
SIXTEENTH CENTURY
ZARAGOZA

PLATE 354

VASE IN THE CATHEDRAL OF EL PILAR
FIFTEENTH CENTURY
ZARAGOZA

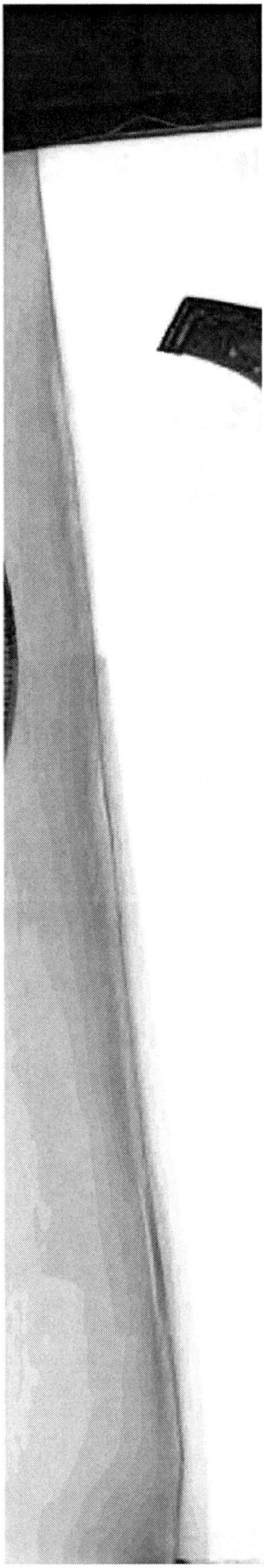

PLATE 351

...E CATHEDRAL OF EL PILAR
...TEENTH CENTURY
ZARAGOZA

PLATE 354

PORTAL OF THE CHURCH OF SAN MIGUEL,
ZARAGOZA

PLATE 355

FAÇADE OF THE CHURCH OF SANTA ENGRACIA
ZARAGOZA

PLATE 356

CHURCH OF ST. PAUL. PUERTA DEL CRISTO
ZARAGOZA

PLATE 335

CHURCH OF SANTA ENGRACIA
ZARAGOZA

PLATE 358

TOWER OF THE CALLE DE ANTONIO PEREZ

PLATE 359

PLATE 360

TOWER OF SAN PABLO
ZARAGOZA

PLATE 361

TOWER OF THE TROVADOR
ZARAGOZA

PLATE 362

ANCIENT WALL AND TOWER, LOOKING NORTH-WEST, FROM THE BRIDGE

PLATE 363

STATUE OF PIGNATELLI
ZARAGOZA

PLATE 364

COURT-YARD IN THE HOUSE OF PARDO
ZARAGOZA

PLATE 365

DETAIL OF THE COURT-YARD IN THE HOUSE OF PARDO
ZARAGOZA

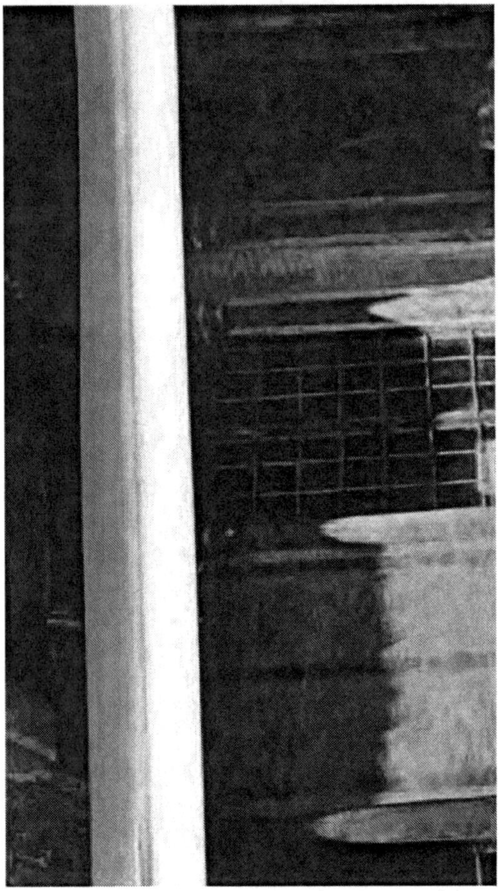

PLATE 367

PALACE OF THE PROVINCIAL DEPUTATION
ZARAGOZA

PLATE 366

ENTRANCE TO THE AUDIENCIA PALACE

PLATE 367

PALACE OF THE PROVINCIAL DEPUTATION

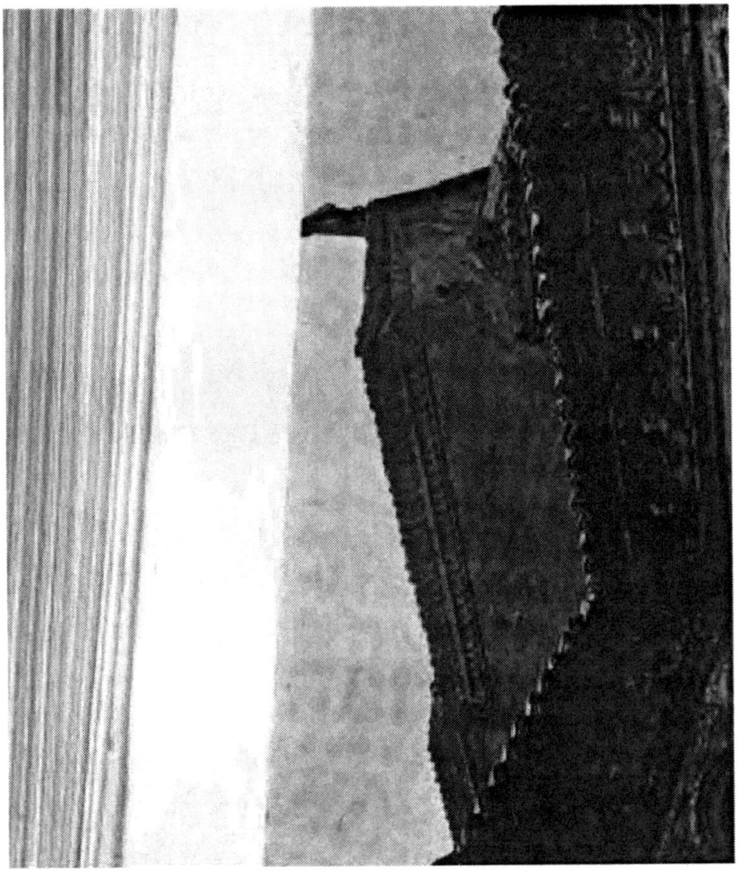

PLATE 369

EAVES ON THE HOUSE OF THE CONDE DE ARGILLO
ZARAGOZA

COURT-YARD IN THE COUNT OF ZARAGOZA

PLATE 371

HOUSE IN THE PLAZA DE SAN CARLOS
ZARAGOZA

PLATE 372

THE EXCHANGE
ZARAGOZA

PLATE 373

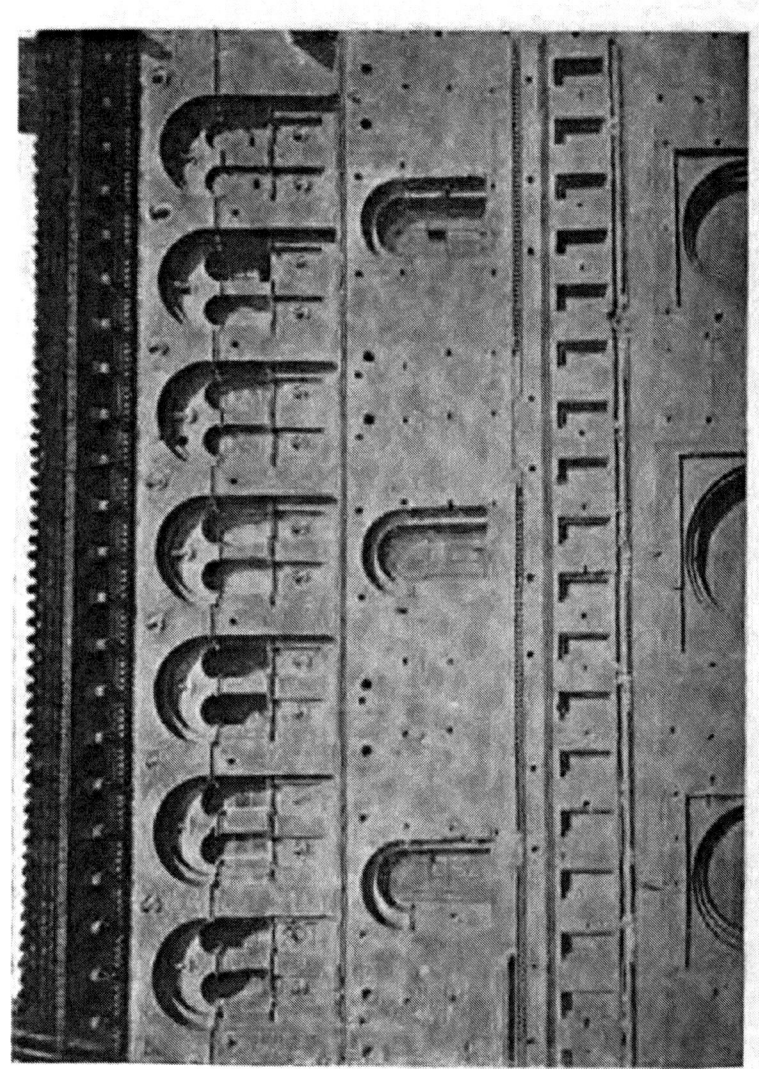

FAÇADE OF THE EXCHANGE
ZARAGOZA

Plate 374

PLATE 375

PORCH OF THE HOUSE OF ZAPORTA; OR, OF THE INFANTA

PLATE 376

COURT-YARD OF THE HOUSE OF ZAPORTA, OR OF THE INFANTA, ZARAGOZA

COURT-YARD OF THE HOUSE OF ZAPORTA; OR, OF THE INFANTA

PLATE 378

PLATE 379

COURT-YARD IN THE HOUSE OF ZAPORTA; OR, OF THE INFANTA
ZARAGOZA

COURTYARD OF THE HOUSE OF ZAPORTA, OR OF THE INFANTA, ZARAGOZA

DETAIL OF THE COURT

PLATE 381

DETAIL OF THE COURT-YARD OF THE HOUSE OF

COURT OF THE BRAVE ITALIAN MAN
ZAR PALACE

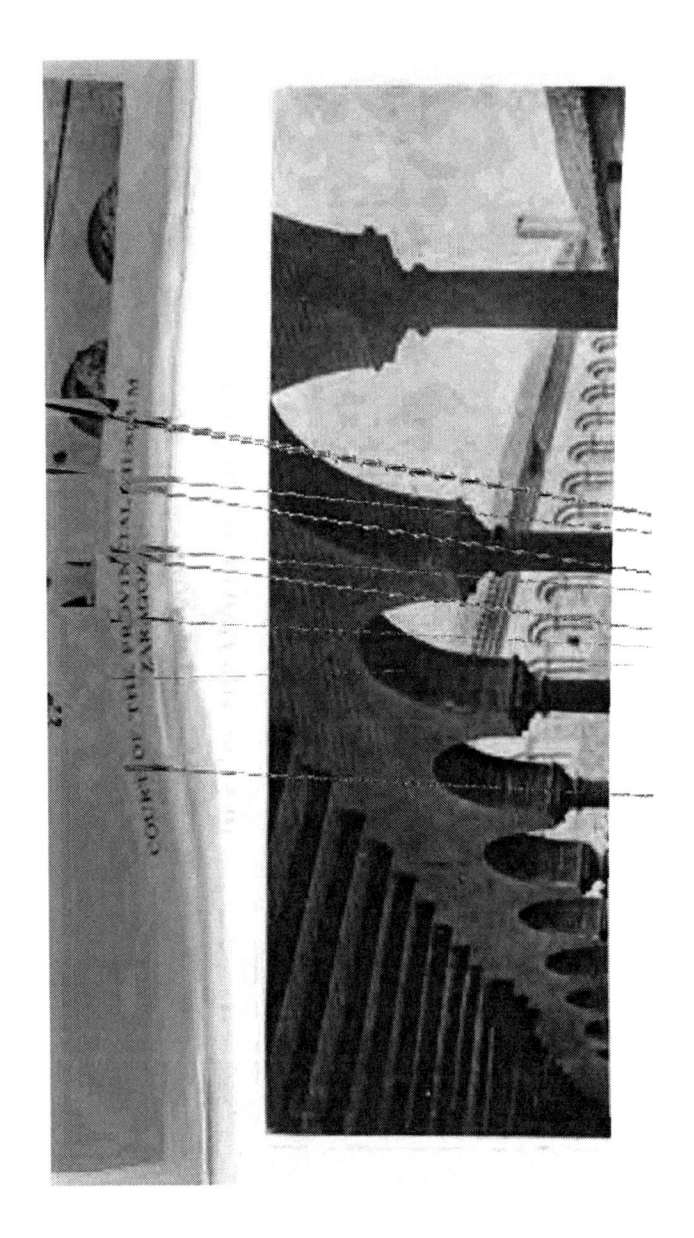

PLATE 383

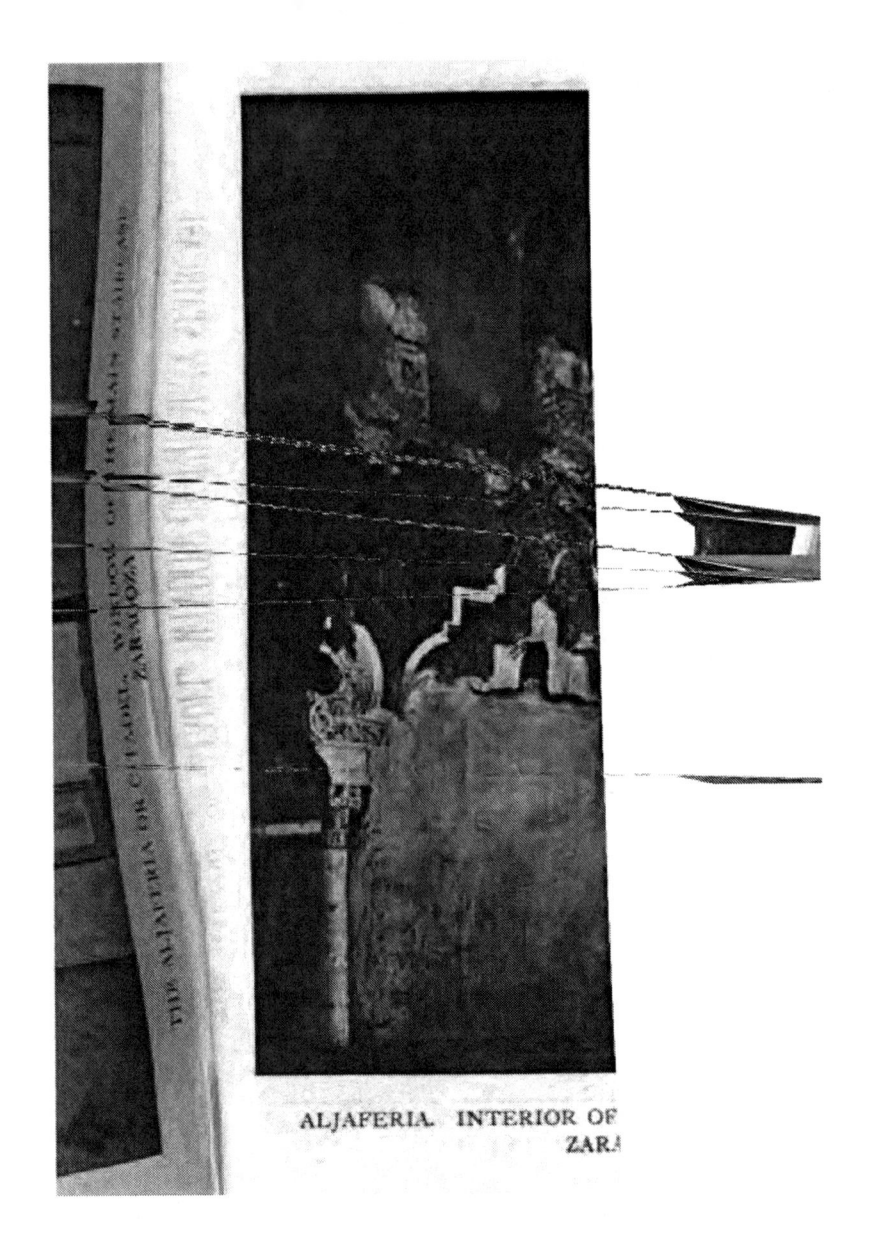

ALJAFERIA. INTERIOR OF THE ALJAFERIA OR CITADEL, WITH LOOK-OUT OF THE HALF-MOON, ZARAGOZA

PLATE 385

ALJAFERIA. INTERIOR OF THE (SO CALLED) MOSQUE
ZARAGOZA

PLATE 386

ALJAFERIA. ENTRANCE TO THE (SO CALLED) MOSQUE
ZARAGOZA

PLATE 387

ALJAFERIA. INTERIOR OF THE (SO CALLED) MOSQUE

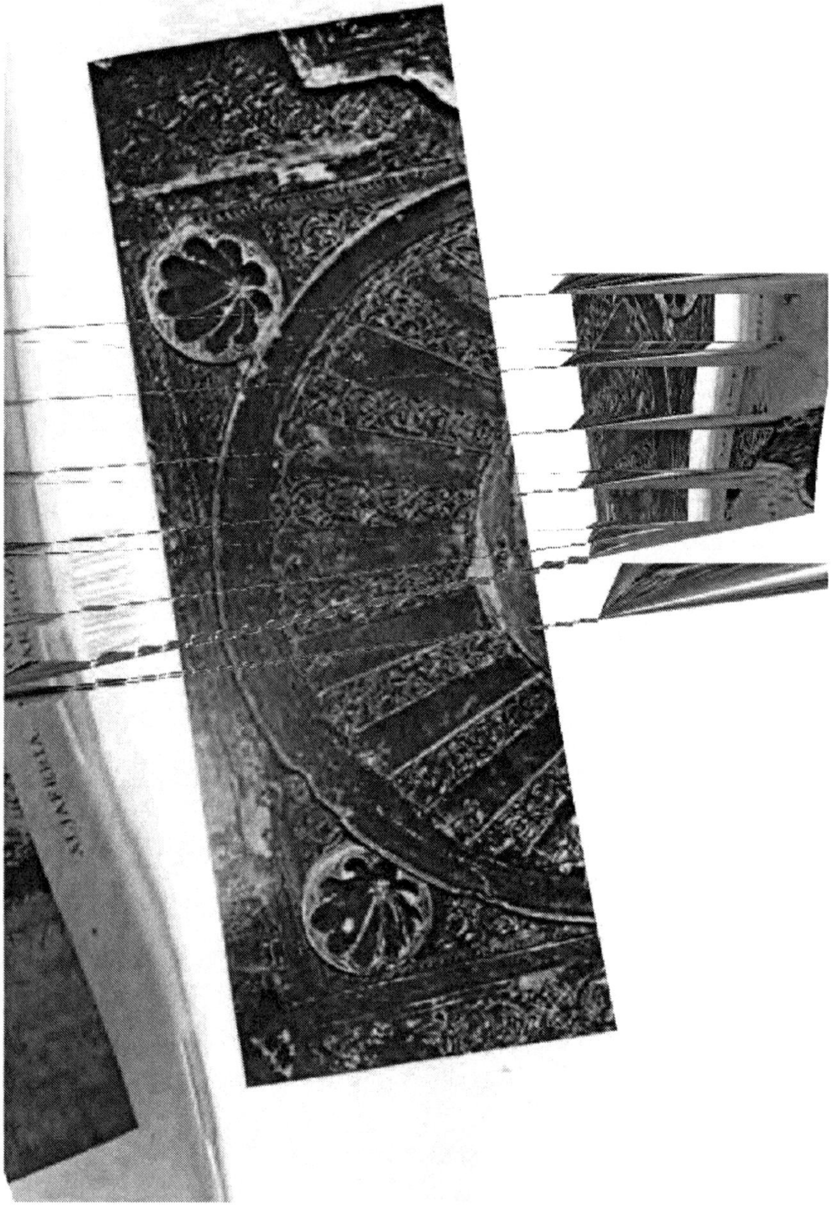

PLATE 389

ALJAFERIA. DETAILS OF THE INTERIOR

PLATE 390

DETAILS OF THE ALJAFERIA
PROVINCIAL MUSEUM, ZARAGOZA

CPSIA information can be obtained at www.ICGtesting.com
Printed in the USA
LVOW051537200212

269545LV00010B/77/P